HOW GRAMMAR W
A Self-Teaching Guide

HOW GRAMMAR WORKS
A Self-Teaching Guide

Patricia Osborn

WILEY

John Wiley & Sons, Inc.

New York   •   Chichester   •   Brisbane   •   Toronto   •   Singapore

Publisher: David Sobel
Editor: Katherine Schowalter
Managing Editor: Frank Grazioli
Editing, Design, and Production: Publication Services, Inc.

Library of Congress Cataloging-in-Publication Data

Osborn, Patricia.
  How grammar works / Patricia Osborn.
    p.   cm.
  Bibliography: p.
  ISBN 0-471-61297-9
    1. English language—Grammar—1950–   I. Title.
PE1112.083   1989
428.2—dc19   88-32267
                             CIP

Printed in the United States of America
89 90 10 9 8 7 6 5 4 3 2

How to Use This Book

This book is designed to guide you step by step through the basics of English grammar. Part One will help you learn to strip a sentence down to its essentials to discover the underlying principles of its grammar. As you work with the examples, you will become familiar with the important relationships among the words at work in every sentence that we speak and write.

The opening chapters of Part One progress from the simple to the complex, yet they present fundamentals of grammar that should become even clearer if you review them after finishing the entire section.

Part Two takes the concepts that you have mastered and builds from this groundwork. As you work in these chapters, maintain the habit of identifying the key elements of every sentence, a basic skill that gains in importance as sentences become more involved and complex.

You will find two types of exercises in this guide. One is especially written as a clear, direct reinforcement of the concept just presented and lets you check your mastery of it. You may choose to write the answers out as a self-test or, if in doubt, review the preceding material to find the answers. You will find a section containing answers in the back of the book.

The second type of exercise consists of writings chosen to give you practice working with selections in a variety of styles and fields. You should not expect 100% accuracy from yourself with these. Their purpose is to help you become more aware of grammar and the value of its application to material encountered outside of a textbook setting.

In working with this guide, concentrate on the work that words actually do in sentences, not on grammatical terms or definitions. Part Two concerns questions of correct usage and ways to become more effective in handling your language. To take full advantage of the examples and exercises, try to understand the reasons underlying each rule and discern how each fits into the total system of grammar.

Your goal—and the goal of this book—is to make you feel comfortable with grammar and the way words work.

SOURCES

Grateful acknowledgment is made to the following:

Pages 10–11: Gerald Durrell, *Golden Bats and Pink Pigeons*, Simon & Schuster, New York, 1977, pp. 127–128.

Page 37: Graham Greene, *The Lawless Roads*, Penguin Books, New York, rpt. 1982, p. 51.

Page 42: Thor Heyerdahl, *The Ra Expeditions*, Doubleday Publishing, New York, pp. 233–234.

Page 48: William L. Shirer, *20th Century Journey*, Little, Brown, Boston, 1985, p. 322.

Pages 55–56: Mark and Delia Owens, *Cry of the Kalahari*, Houghton Mifflin, Boston, 1984, pp. 43–44 and 46.

Page 57: Zora Neale Hurston, *Their Eyes Were Watching God*, University of Illinois Press, Urbana, 1965, pp. 231–234.

Page 88: Elinor Wylie, "Sea Lullaby," in *Collected Poems of Elinor Wylie*, Alfred A. Knopf, New York, 1932.

Pages 112–113: Frank Marshall Davis, "Four Glimpses of Night," in *Black Voices*, Abraham Chapman, Ed., Mentor, New York, 1968, p. 434.

Pages 123–124: John Steinbeck, *Of Mice and Men*, Viking Press, New York, 1937, rpt. 1965, pp. 23–24.

Page 126: James Fenimore Cooper, *The Deerslayer*, New American Library, New York, 1963, p. 312.

Page 126: Anne Tyler, *The Accidental Tourist*, Alfred A. Knopf, New York, 1985, p. 312.

Pages 147–148: F. Scott Fitzgerald, *The Great Gatsby*, Charles Scribner's Sons, New York, 1925, p. 40.

Pages 148–149: Charles Dickens, *Hard Times*, New American Library, New York, pp. 30–31.

Page 149: Robert Claiborne, *Our Marvelous Native Tongue*, Times Books, New York, 1983, p. 181.

Page 149: Daniel J. Boorstin, *The Discoverers*, Random House, New York, 1983, p. 484.

Pages 187–188: Richard P. Feynman, *Surely You're Joking, Mr. Feynman!* W. W. Norton, New York, 1985, p. 256.

Page 191: Edna O'Brien, "Sleepwalking at the Ritz," in *Condé Nast's Traveler*, June 1988, p. 116.

Page 192: Henry I. Kurtz, "Dime-Store Doughboys," *American Heritage*, December 1986, p. 75.

Page 192: John Berger, "The Credible Word," *Threepenny Review*, Winter 1988 (reprinted by *Harper's Magazine*, July 1988, p. 35).

Contents

PART I
THE ESSENTIALS OF GRAMMAR

1 People Invent Language 3
Language Is a Tool 3
What Is Grammar, Anyway? 3

2 Nouns: The Building Blocks of Language 7
Words Work Magic Spells 7
How Does Language Work, and Why? 7
Baby Talk Makes Sense 8
What Is a Noun? 9
Questions Nouns Answer 9
Practice 10
The Useful Word *The* 11
Two More Determiners: *A* and *An* 12
Practice 13

3 The Subject: What It's All About 15
Getting to the Subject 15
How Nouns Work as Subjects 16
Practice 16

4 Verbs: The Energy of Sentences 17
What Do Verbs Say? 17
How Do Subjects and Verbs Work Together? 18
The First Step in Grammar 19
Practice 20

5 Tense: How Verbs Tell Time 21
The Three Principal Parts 21
The Parts of Verbs at Work 22
Irregular Verbs 23
Practice 25
Do You Use "Good Grammar"? 25
Practice 25

6   Complements: The Completion of the Verb   29
Transitive Verbs   30
Intransitive Verbs   30
Linking Verbs   31
Practice   31

7   Pronouns   33
Speaking Personally   33
How Pronouns Express Person and Number   34
Practice   36

8   Adjectives: The First Add-On   39
How Adjectives Modify   39
How to Find an Adjective   40
Adjective or Noun?   41
Adjectives that Limit by Number   41
Practice   42

9   Adverbs: Add-On #2   43
Adverbs that Modify Verbs   43
How Words Work   45
Adverbs that Modify Adjectives   45
Adverbs that Modify Adverbs   46
Practice   48

10   Prepositions: Relating One Word to Another   49
Can We Get Along Without Prepositions?   49
Prepositions in Action   49
Prepositional Phrases as Adjectives   51
Practice   52
Prepositional Phrases as Adverbs   53
Practice   53
Some Advice About Usage   54
When Is a "Preposition" Not a Preposition?   54
Practice   55

11   Coordinating Conjunctions: One and One Make Two   57
And: The Most Common Conjunction   57
Compound Sentences, Compound Parts   59
How to Be Sure What *And* Joins   60
Compound Parts in a Series   60
Practice   61
More Coordinating Conjunctions   62
Paired Conjunctions   63
Practice   64

A Note About Punctuation 64

The Eight Parts of Speech 67

PART II
ACTION AND INTERACTION:
THE SYSTEM AT WORK

12 Word Order Is Part of Meaning 71
Subjects Naturally Come First 71
Judging Sentences by Purpose 72
Practice 74
Changing Word Order Changes Purpose 75
Practice 77

13 Just Enough Punctuation 79
Punctuating Sentences 79
Punctuating Within Sentences 81
Keeping Punctuation Clean 83

14 The 5 W's and an H 85
Active Reading 85
Grammar in Action 86
Practice (with Poetry) 87
Putting Your Knowledge of Grammar to Work 89

15 The Amazing Word *Be* and Its Many Faces 91
A Defective Verb 91
Uses of *Be* 92
Practice 95
Progressive Verb Phrases 95
Practice 97
The Passive Voice 97
Practice 99

16 More about Nouns and Pronouns 101
Cases 101
Practice 105
More Practice 105
Possessives 106

17 Introducing the Verbals: The Participles Are Coming! 109
The Participles Have Come! 109
Participles as Adjectives 110
Participial Phrases 110

Practice   111
Participles in Action   112
The Gerund: Another Versatile Verbal   113
Practice   114
To Be or Not to Be: The Infinitive   115
Practice   118

**18   More Punctuation: I Said, "May I Have
Your Attention, Please?"   121**
How Quotation Marks Work   121
Reading Dialogue   123
Quotation Marks in Action   123
Practice   124
More Ways to Use Quotation Marks   124
Italic Letters   125
The Colon   125
Today's Punctuation   127

19   How Sentences Combine   129
Complex Sentences   129
Subordinating Conjunctions   130
Adverb Clauses   130
Practice   131
Practice   132
The Adjective Clause   132
Practice   137
Practice   138
The Noun Clause   139
Practice   143

**20   Keeping It Simple,
Even When Sentences Get Complex   145**
What "Good" Is a Complex Sentence?   145
The Sound of Language   146
Grammar in Action   148
What Makes Grammar Important?   149

21   Verbs Do More: The Fine Points of Using Verbs   151
Verbs Have Their Moods   152
Practice   154
Common Verbs that Cause Great Confusion   155
Practice   156
One Negative Is Enough   159
Be Careful of "Of"   160
Practice   160

Splitting Infinitives   160
Making Perfect Use of the Perfect Tenses   161

22   Questions of Usage: How Can Words Agree with One Another When People Don't Agree?   163
Indefinite Pronouns and Nouns   164
Demonstrative Pronouns and Adjectives   167
Practice   168
Compound Personal Pronouns   168
Agreement Between Subject and Verb   170

23   Forming Comparisons Correctly: A Matter of Degree   175
The Three Degrees of Comparison   176
Tips for "Perfect" Usage   177
How the Comparative and Superlative Degrees Work   178
Practice   179

24   How to Make Yourself More Effective in English   181
Seven Key Steps to Better Usage   181

25   The Complete Sentence: Putting It All Together   185
Ellipses   185
Keep It Simple   187
What Is a Sentence Fragment?   188
Qualities that Count in Writing Good Sentences   189
Samples of Today's Good Writing   191

Appendix   195

Index   203

HOW GRAMMAR WORKS
A Self-Teaching Guide

PART I

THE ESSENTIALS OF GRAMMAR

INTRODUCTION

Grammar goes beyond rules and definitions. It is a study of the system that powers one of our most useful and often-used inventions—language. Understanding grammar can put you more in control of your language and help you become more effective when you speak, write, and even read.

The aim of this book is to help you discover how the elements of English grammar work so that the rules for usage don't seem senseless and random, but necessary parts of a smooth-functioning whole. It has been written with the belief that a study of grammar will prove both helpful and interesting as you become more aware of the endless possibilities of the English language and the superbly direct system of word order generating its power.

It is hoped that *How Grammar Works* will provide the foundation you need to put grammar successfully to work for you.

Chapter 1

People Invent Language

LANGUAGE IS A TOOL

Early people invented language, just as we have had to invent all of our other tools. Almost all inventions are attempts to improve our quality of life, and language is no different. As the world becomes more complex, the tool of language adapts and changes with it.

No one questions the importance of language. It's very different with grammar.

WHAT IS GRAMMAR, ANYWAY?

Isn't it a set of rules to learn and follow so that you can speak correctly and write better? Actually, no.

Grammar is really an analysis of language. It's a study of how a language works. Like a technical manual, a grammar guide provides a breakdown of our language, showing how its various parts operate and how they fit together into sentences. Just as knowledge about the operation of one combustion engine will teach you the principle behind all combustion engines, so a study of grammar teaches you the basic construction and operation of all sentences.

Even as they grow more complicated, they still operate on the same principle. Using language is like driving a car. When you drive, you think about the road, the traffic, and the place you are going. As you drive along, you don't have to remind your hands to steer or your feet to press the proper pedal. If you did, you'd freeze at the steering wheel. There is too much going on at once. To a driver, operating a car becomes automatic.

It is much the same with language. When you talk, you don't think in terms of using grammar. You think about ideas, about what you want to say. Your mind is not on the process but on the goal you want to reach with your words.

You can be a good driver without being able to name all the parts of an engine and explain how they work, but knowledge of a car's mechanical system helps you to understand its performance and judge its response. An engineer diagrams the mechanical system of an automobile to show its parts and their relationship to one another. In the same way, a grammatical diagram shows the parts of a sentence and their relationship (see Figure 1-1). Both diagrams serve a similar purpose.

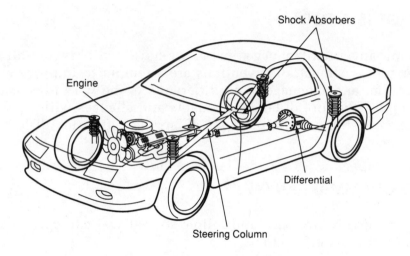

The clause

A COMPOUND–COMPLEX SENTENCE
When you check the diagram of a sentence, you discover the relationship of its parts, and their function becomes clearer.

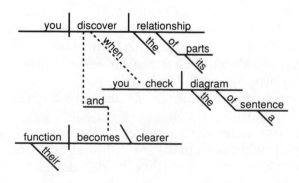

Figure 1-1

Understanding the system that makes English work—its grammar—can help you gain control over your language. It helps you spot and label problems in your speech and writing.

A study of grammar provides an "inside" understanding of language. You learn what the parts of a sentence are designed to do and why. This discovery enables you to cut directly through to the "meat" of a sentence and thus helps you become a more effective reader.

Knowledge of grammar, then, gives you greater control of your language when you read, speak, or write.

Chapter 2

Nouns:
The Building Blocks
of Language

Because people invented language in times so long ago, it's sometimes treated like something holy or even magic. From the beginning, in fact, people have used words not simply as tools, but as ways to gain and hold power.

WORDS WORK MAGIC SPELLS

In a world without words, early people lived in darkness and fear. They had no way to explain the causes of thunder, fire, sickness, sunsets, and comets.

After the invention of language, some claimed to know the secrets of the universe and the magic spells that would make the gods less angry. Today we call this belief in magic superstition, but the high priests' and sorcerers' command of language gave them power. Primitive people looked up to such men and called them wise.

There is, however, no real secret to language. Babies learn it almost without effort. Its basic principles are really very simple, and they form the framework of grammar.

HOW DOES LANGUAGE WORK, AND WHY?

Let's look at how a baby learns to speak. Babies seem to follow the same steps that early people must have taken to invent a language.

What are some of the first words that a baby learns?

Mama
Daddy
Baby
Cookie

First come the important people or things in its life. To a baby, words such as *bowwow* and *ticktock* do not mean sounds; we use them as names for *dog* and *clock* because they have a "singsong" sound that babies like and find easy to imitate.

Tourists in a foreign country also need the names of things first. They want to know how to say *restaurant*, *beer*, *elevator*, *money*.

In the same way, early people must have made up names for *deer*, *wolf*, or *danger* among the first words in their new invention, language.

BABY TALK MAKES SENSE

Baby talk shows how you can make yourself understood quite well, even if your language is limited to names of things, or *nouns*, as they are called in a study of grammar.

Here are examples of baby talk, using only names (nouns). Is there any doubt what Baby is trying to say?

- cookie
- Baby, cookie
- Mama, cookie, baby
- Cookie, floor

This experiment won't work with other kinds or classes of words, only with nouns (or names).

For example, try these.

- under, in, above
- and, while, although
- drive, burn

None of these sets of words seems to have a special sense when taken together as a sentence.

Now, try these nouns.

- baseball, window, lamp
- lightning, barn, fire
- terrorists, airplane, hostages

Is there any question that a definite idea connects each set of three nouns? What words would you add to turn them into complete sentences? You can easily see how nouns or names are the building blocks of language. Nouns are also a key to understanding when we read.

WHAT IS A NOUN?

A noun belongs to a class of words that name a person, place, action, quality—anything for which people have needed to invent a name.

Concrete nouns name what can actually be sensed. For example, all the following underlined words are concrete nouns:

We see a <u>man</u>,
we taste <u>food</u>,
we hear <u>music</u>,
we smell <u>smoke</u>,
we feel a <u>shiver</u>,
go up our <u>spine</u>.

Abstract nouns name qualities not directly sensed. Examples:

freedom,
success,
pride,
happiness

QUESTIONS NOUNS ANSWER

Remember, since a noun is a name, it will always answer the questions *who?* or *what?*

Who is talking?

a *man*
Larry
the *parrot*
a *ghost*

What is your favorite subject?

science	*food*
politics	*sports*

What do you want most in life?

> *freedom*
> *money*
> *success*
> *happiness*

Each of the listed words answers the question *who* or *what*. Each one is a noun, although some do not name something solid that you can point to and see.

Which would you say are concrete nouns and which abstract? Although some can be judged either way, there is no question that all are nouns.

Note: Words like *you* or *it* do not actually *name* someone or something and are therefore not nouns.

PRACTICE

Read the following paragraph and list, in order, the nouns that you find. Remember, a noun is a naming word that answers the questions *who?* or *what?* in a sentence. **Warning:** Some may be tricky because much depends on *how* a word works in a sentence.

Compare these two sentences:

a. The house is big.
b. The house payment is big.

What is big? In a, *house* answers the question and is therefore a noun. In b, *payment* is the answer and the noun. *House* tells "What payment?" not "What?"

The following selection is adapted from a paragraph by naturalist Gerald Durrell in *Golden Bats and Pink Pigeons*. As you read it, don't be surprised if you aren't sure whether some words are nouns. For now, it is important only to get a feeling for nouns and to become aware that names—or nouns—are what the selection is really all about.

A WORLD OF WONDERS

Any naturalist at certain moments has experienced a thrill at the beauty and complexity of life, and a feeling of depression that one lifetime is an unfairly short span in such a paradise of wonders as the world is. You get this feeling when, for the first time, you see the beauty, variety, and lushness of a tropical rain forest, with its maze of a thousand different trees, each bedecked with gardens of orchids, enmeshed in a web of creepers. There are so many species that you cannot believe that number of different forms have evolved. You feel it when you see for the first time a great congregation of mammals living together or a vast, restless conglomeration of birds. You feel it when you see a butterfly or a dragonfly emerge from its cocoon. . . . when you first see a stick or a leaf turn into an insect, or a piece of dappled shade into a herd of zebras. You feel it when you see a gigantic school of dolphins stretching as far as the eye can see, rocking and leaping joyously through their blue world; or a tiny spider manufacturing from its body a transparent, seemingly unending line that will act as a transport as it sets out on its aerial exploration of its world.

(This passage contains 53 nouns in all. For answers, see page 195.)

TIP: After you have identified the nouns, reread the paragraph. Try to leap from noun to noun, over the connecting words. See how your mind "fills in" many of the ideas, just as it did with the sample sets of nouns used earlier as examples.

Making nouns a main target can help you become a faster, better reader.

THE USEFUL WORD *THE*

Not sure whether a word is a noun? Even though all nouns answer the questions *who* or *what*, sometimes you want to be doubly certain.

The word *the* can help you check. Test the would-be noun in a little sentence of four words. Use *the* as the first word and put the supposed noun right after it.

How *The* Works:

The _____ is _____.

Try it out with *sky* and *under*.

The _____ sky _____ is _____ blue _____.
(This makes sense. *Sky* is a noun.)
The _____ under _____ is _____ down _____.
(Just plain nonsense. *Under* is not a noun.)

Why *The* Works

It works because *the* is a **determiner**, or indicator, of a noun. This means it's like a signpost that alerts you a noun will follow. Of course, *the* doesn't have to be used every time you use a noun. For example:

- Kittens are cute.
- The kittens are cute.

How do the two sentences differ in meaning? As you see, the word *the* not only signals a noun, but carries a special idea as well.

Sometimes other words separate the word *the* from its noun. This makes it even more important as a signal that a noun is coming soon.

- The three tiny kittens are cute and fluffy.

How *The* Works as a Check for Nouns

Which of the underlined words in the following sentences is not a noun?

1. The <u>volume</u> is loud.
2. The <u>solution</u> is obvious.
3. The <u>invisible</u> is small.

Clearly, *the invisible* doesn't make sense, so *invisible* is not a noun in sentence 3.

TWO MORE DETERMINERS: *A* AND *AN*

Like *the*, the words *a* and *an* are signals of a noun. Compare:

- A tree provides shade.
- The tree provides shade.

How are their meanings different?

Note: *An* is used before words beginning with vowels a, e, i, o, and u (such as *airplane*, *engine*, *oven*) or vowel sounds (such as *hour*) to make them easier to say.

PRACTICE

By using *the* as a determiner, check out the following words to see if they can be used as nouns. Put them in test sentences of four words, as in the examples.

The _____ is _____.

Label a word *noun* if it makes sense as part of your sentence and *other* if it doesn't.

1. arena	11. revolution	21. without
2. interview	12. sugary	22. kind
3. belief	13. enemy	23. matter
4. unfair	14. opening	24. magnetic
5. peace	15. glamorous	25. passenger
6. incredible	16. Seattle	26. menu
7. creature	17. found	27. future
8. program	18. perhaps	28. feeling
9. advantage	19. reasonable	29. join
10. near	20. trick	30. Napoleon

MORE TO KNOW: With nouns such as *Mr. Jackson* or *Oregon*, you must think of what the word really names before you check it out. That is, Mr. Jackson is *the* man, and Oregon is *the* state.

Nouns that name a particular person, place, or thing are called **proper nouns** and should begin with a capital letter.

(For answers, see page 195.)

Chapter 3

The Subject:
What It's All About

- Family, Vacation, Rome

It's not hard to see how these three words, all nouns, make sense together. What words would you add to turn them into an ordinary sentence? Here are some possible ways to do it. Would yours be the same?

- The family spent its vacation in Rome.
- My family took a vacation and went to Rome.
- Our family went on vacation to Rome.

As you see, the three sentences say almost the same thing. Nouns alone made the meaning quite obvious. While it's not always this clear, it is true that nouns are the building blocks of a sentence.

GETTING TO THE SUBJECT

One noun has a special job in all three examples. It is the word naming *who* or *what* the sentence is about. To find the right one, ask yourself, "Who or what is doing something in the sentence?" Clearly, *family* is the answer.

When we label them as **parts of speech**, words like *family* are called nouns with reference to the kind of ideas they contain. For example, nouns give everybody and everything a name. A noun can also be identified by its specific use in a sentence.

HOW NOUNS WORK AS SUBJECTS

Words do added work when they're combined into a sentence. In all three examples, the word *family* does the same job. It serves as the **subject** of the sentence.

> The **subject**
> is a word that tells
> *who* or *what*
> a sentence is about.

In this case, the subject is the noun, *family*.

Of course, the other two nouns could be the subjects of their own sentences, too.

- Their vacation lasted three weeks.
- Rome is the capital of Italy.

It doesn't take a long definition or difficult formula to pick out the subject. You just have to ask yourself a couple of simple questions.

> To find the subject
> **ask:**
> who or what
> is the sentence about?
> *Who* or *What*
> is doing something in the sentence?

PRACTICE

What noun acts as the subject of each of the following sentences?

1. The clown was wearing a bright orange wig.
2. The leader of the band gave the downbeat.
3. A good friend can be trusted.
4. Yolanda is my best friend.
5. The weather looked good for our barbecue.
6. After reviewing the evidence, the judge gave a verdict of not guilty.
7. Without a doubt, Crenshaw deserves credit for quick thinking.

(For answers, see page 195.)

Chapter 4

Verbs: The Energy of Sentences

WHAT DO VERBS SAY?

- Took, Went

Standing by themselves, verbs don't carry meaning as solidly as nouns, the building blocks of a sentence. What kind of sentences would you write using the two words *took* and *went*, both of which are verbs?

- Tom took a taxi and went to the airport.
- Terry took the ball and went for a touchdown.
- Todd took the wrong advice and went bankrupt.

When a set of verbs, rather than a set of nouns, is listed together, there's no way to figure out a single idea behind them that everyone might think of immediately.

The two essential parts of every good sentence are an *actor* plus an *action*.

The part of speech that expresses what action the subject (actor) does is called a **verb**.

Verbs can express a lot of action:

- The grasshopper <u>leaped</u>.

Or the act of being:

- God <u>is</u>.

Or whatever else a subject does, is doing, or did:

- Supper <u>smells</u> delicious.

HOW DO SUBJECTS AND VERBS WORK TOGETHER?

- The subject is what a sentence is about. The verb is what drives it.

You might think of it in electrical terms. The verb is the source of energy; verbs send out the power that enables the message to come through.

To find the verb, first, find the subject. Ask, "*Who* or *what* is the sentence about?" Then, name the subject and ask, "*Did* what?" or "*Does* what?"

Sentences may seem long and complicated at first, but they all can be reduced to these two basic parts:

Somebody or something (1. **the subject**)
Does something (2. **the verb**)

All the other words in the sentence radiate from and relate to this core.

You really need just two words to have a perfectly good sentence, if one is the subject and the other its verb:

- Cathy smiled.
- Leaves fell.
- The dog barked. (*The* is a determiner. You can also say, "Dogs bark.")
- Maxwell ran.
- The man confessed.

You can add more words to any of these sentences if you wish, but the resulting sentences will still boil down to the same two words: the subject and verb.

For example, read the following sentences. See how the same subjects and verbs are at work here as in the preceding five short sentences. In spite of all the added words, the actor/action are the same.

- Cathy smiled at the thought of her exciting plans for a ski trip to Colorado.
- Leaves in colors of gold, rust, and bronze fell from the tree to cover the ground.
- The huge dog tied in the front yard of the house barked at everyone and everything passing by.
- Losing his nerve completely, Maxwell ran at the sight of the hairy creature hiding beneath the bushes.
- The man caught by the police in the carryout confessed to robbing eight other stores in the past month.

Although you add more words, the facts in the case haven't changed:

(The) Man confessed.

To find the facts you need to identify the subject and verb first.

All Sentences Work the Same Way

No matter how long or how difficult a sentence looks, the most important words are always:

The Main Subject:
(Who or what the sentence is about) and
The Main Verb:
(What the subject did or does)

THE FIRST STEP IN GRAMMAR

What is the secret of being good at grammar? No matter what else you are asked to do, *first* look for the subject and verb. This lets you find your way around in any sentence.

The subject and verb come before everything else in grammar since they alone are the two basic parts to a sentence. It's like being sure to look for the direction North when you study a map or checking the area code before you make a long-distance phone call.

Whether it's done consciously or unconsciously, everyone who is good at grammar picks out the subject and verb almost automatically. When you have a problem understanding something that seems hard to read, it is often helpful to search consciously for these two basic elements. It doesn't pay to ignore the *subject* and *verb:* they're really what a sentence is all about!

To find the subject and verb
always ask the following questions:

Subject   Who? What?
Verb   Did what? Does what?

1. Such words as *no, never, always,* and *really* are never part of the verb.
2. A verb form with *to* in front of it is never part of the *subject + verb.*

Example: He likes to go.
To go is not a verb.

3. After you pick out the subject and verb, read them together. If they are right, they will make sense. They will either form a perfectly good sentence or need only one other word to complete their meaning.

PRACTICE

Identify the subjects and verbs that form the core of the following sentences.

1. More passengers crammed into the crowded elevator.
2. Most members of the park board disagreed with the chairman's proposal.
3. In her speech, the candidate promised not to increase taxes.
4. The sudden noise in the hallway startled everyone in the room.
5. Surprisingly few experts correctly predicted the outcome of the election.
6. The player hurtled over the goal line for the winning touchdown.
7. Without a moment's hesitation, Jensen leaped into the raging waters.

(For answers, see page 195.)

Chapter 5

Tense: How Verbs Tell Time

What's the difference between *run* and *walk*? The question is not so silly as it first sounds. In grammar, there is no difference in their use in sentences. Both can work as verbs. To find their difference in meaning, you'd look in the dictionary.

But what's the difference between *walk* and *walked*? between *run* and *ran*? You won't find these questions answered by their definitions. Along with its dictionary meaning, every verb carries other ideas that we grasp instantly because of the form it takes. This fact makes verbs both the hardest working and most complicated parts of the English language.

THE THREE PRINCIPAL PARTS OF VERBS

To help us express these tenses, every verb has three principal parts.

- Walk, walked, walked

They are used to form the three tenses, or times, that verbs express:

Present
Past
Future

Yes, the second and third parts of *walk* are exactly alike; therefore, it belongs to the class of **regular verbs**.

Regular verbs add *-ed* to their basic form:

aim	aimed	aimed
call	called	called
laugh	laughed	laughed
smell	smelled	smelled
play	played	played

If a verb is regular, the dictionary does not show how to form its other principal parts. It's taken for granted you'll add *-ed*.

Some *-ed* verbs vary slightly. Many other verbs use the same *-ed* sound as a tense signal, but need a change in spelling to make them easier to pronounce correctly. These include such verbs as:

try	tried	tried
cry	cried	cried
phone	phoned	phoned
vote	voted	voted
drop	dropped	dropped
pop	popped	popped

Since their spelling can cause problems, the dictionary helps by listing all parts of verbs such as these.

THE PARTS OF VERBS AT WORK

Alone or with helpers, the principal parts of verbs carry a sense of time along with the action or act of being that they express.

Primary Tenses

> PRESENT: Today, I <u>call</u>.
> PAST: Yesterday, I <u>called</u>.
> FUTURE: Tomorrow, I <u>will call</u>.

Perfect Tenses

> PRESENT PERFECT: Before now, I <u>have called</u>.
> PAST PERFECT: In the past, I <u>had called</u>.
> FUTURE PERFECT: By some future date, I <u>will have called</u>.

Why are the perfect tenses called "perfect"? Anything perfect is complete, and the perfect tenses stress an action at its completion. Here's an example of both the tense and the word *perfect* at work as a verb.

- The mad scientist *has perfected* a formula for turning himself into a dragonfly.

IRREGULAR VERBS

Forming primary and perfect tenses with regular verbs is easy. In fact, it's so easy that it seems foolish to say there are second and third parts, when both are alike. A major difficulty of the English language becomes clearer when you meet the irregular verbs.

First, check out the three principal parts of a few of them.

go	went	gone
do	did	done
sink	sank	sunk
think	thought	thought
ring	rang	rung
sing	sang	sung
bring	brought	brought
teach	taught	taught
reach	reached	reached*

* . . . and a regular verb, at last!

Why isn't it "bring, brang, brung"? Or "teach, teached, teached"? Or, for that matter, "reach, raught, raught"? A look at the differences among a few irregular verbs tells the story. Today's English is a juicy stew of words, taken from many tongues and times. Many still follow patterns of their mother grammars, but they are so common in English that we hardly notice how irregular they are.

The importance of knowing the three principal parts becomes clear when you chart irregular verbs.

Primary Tenses

PRESENT:	Today, I go.	I write.
PAST:	Yesterday, I went.	I wrote.
FUTURE:	Tomorrow, I will go.	I will write.

Perfect Tenses

PRESENT PERFECT:	I have gone.	I have written.
PAST PERFECT:	I had gone.	I had written.
FUTURE PERFECT:	I will have gone.	I will have written.

Note: Helpers such as *will*, *have*, *had*, and *will have* constitute an important part of the verb. When identifying the main verb in a sentence, always include the base word *plus* all of its helpers.

Auxiliary Verbs

I go. I may go. I can go.
I might have gone. I should have gone.
I would have been gone. I must go. I do go.
I did go.

Each of these sentences uses a form of the word *go*, but helping verbs give a different sense to each version. Helping verbs, also called **auxiliary verbs**, are an essential part of the whole. Be sure to include them along with the "action" form, which always comes last in a verb string.

Notice how a single complete verb can be just one word—*go*—or can have as many as four different words included in its string, as in *would have been gone*.

Helping verbs help express

Tense: will, have, has, had, have been, has been, will have been
Possibility: may, can, could, would, should, might
Ongoing action: am, is, are, was, were
Emphasis: do, does, did

Note: You have already seen how helping verbs work in the future and perfect tenses. You'll learn more ways they help in later chapters.

Some verbs can be used as auxiliary verbs and can work as main verbs, too. For example:

Glen *has* the map.
Iris *did* the artwork.

And some can have their own helpers:

Glenn *might have* the map.
Iris *will do* the artwork.

PRACTICE

Name the three principal parts of the following verbs. Remember, the fact that two base verbs sound alike doesn't mean that they follow the same pattern. If you aren't careful, reciting principal parts of verbs turns into a singsong chant, which results in some silly-sounding mistakes.

If you're not sure about any of the following, the answer is in the dictionary.

1. break	11. jab	21. say
2. build	12. know	22. shine
3. buy	13. leave	23. shrink
4. catch	14. lay	24. sleep
5. drive	15. make	25. speak
6. eat	16. meet	26. steal
7. fly	17. put	27. swear
8. grow	18. ride	28. take
9. hide	19. rise	29. tell
10. imply	20. run	30. whistle

DO YOU USE "GOOD GRAMMAR"?

To get credit for knowing good grammar, be careful about choosing the right principal part of the verb. Don't, for instance, use the past participle to express the simple past tense. This is one of the problem spots that cause people to think someone "doesn't know grammar" or "sounds illiterate."

Just as important, try not to use forms that aren't in the dictionary, such as "brung" in place of *brought*, "knowed" for *knew*, "busted" for *burst*, and "drug" for *dragged*.

PRACTICE

From the choices in parenthesis, pick the one that best fits the time sense of each sentence.

Look for helping verbs (*have*, *has*, *had*, and *will have*) of the perfect tenses. They signal that the right choice is the third principal part of the verb.

1. The lake has _____ over early this year. (freeze, froze, frozen)
2. Soon we will _____ to see the results of our work. (begin, began, begun)

3. The person ahead of me _____ the biggest piece of pie. (choose, chose, chosen)

4. The strong winds had _____ the tree limb down. (blow, blew, blown)

5. Last night, Steve _____ a surprise party for Jennie. (throw, threw, thrown)

6. A vacation often _____ you a new outlook on life. (gives, gave, given)

7. The battered old car had _____ many miles of travel. (see, saw, seen)

8. After the race, Chet _____ thirstily from the thermos. (drink, drank, drunk)

9. A large crate had _____ from the truck onto the roadway. (fall, fell, fallen)

10. I often _____ to the Auto Show. I first _____ in 1984, and I have _____ every year since. (come, came, come)

(For answers, see page 195.)

How Verbs Agree with Their Subjects

Every verb needs a subject, and you've seen the six tenses at work, using *I* as the subject.

With just one exception, they work in the same way with any subject. But the exception is an important one, in both present and present perfect tenses: Verbs agree with their subjects in person and number. *Number* means either singular or plural:

SINGULAR: naming a single thing, such as *box, baby, comet, gorilla*.
PLURAL: naming two or more things, such as *boxes, babies, comets, gorillas*.

With verbs in the present tense, a final -s stands for singular third person. When the subject is a singular noun or *he*, *she*, or *it* (pronouns in third person), a verb in the present tense needs a final -s to show its agreement. Compare the following:

Present Tense

Singular Third Person: A customer calls; duty calls; he, she, or it calls.
Plural and Other Persons: Customers call; duties call; I call; you call; we call; they call.

Present Perfect Tense

Singular Third Person: A customer has called; he, she, or it has called.
Plural and Other Persons: Customers have called; I have called; you have called; they have called.

(See Chapter 7 for a discussion of the concept of person.)

Most babies learn how verbs agree, just by listening. At first, they say:

"Baby want cookie."

Then they learn:

"I want a cookie" and "Daddy loves Baby."
He loves Baby.
The baby wants a cookie.

Note: A few irregular verbs, such as *do* and *go*, add *-es*.

For example: I go, she goes.
You do, he does.

Special points about agreement of subjects and verbs will be discussed in later chapters.

Chapter 6

Complements:
The Completion
of the Verb

It's obvious that verbs are the part of speech that makes sentences "go."

1. They show the action of the subject.
2. They express tense, or relative time: past, present, or future.

Some sentences are complete in themselves with just a subject and a verb.

- An eagle soars.
- The sun has risen.
- Our team will win.

The pattern of these sentences is

Actor + Action
(Subject/Verb)

Some verbs carry action from the subject to a goal. The subjects and verbs of these sentences leave you up in the air. They need an additional word to answer the questions *Who* or *What*? For example:

Terry hit _____?_____.
Stan saw _____?_____.
Cassie made _____?_____.

These sentences don't make complete sense without a word to fill in the blank. That word is called a **complement** because it completes the meaning of the verb.

Terry hit _____what?_____
        the target?
        his elbow?
        the jackpot?

In the blank space goes a word to answer the question *who* or *what*.

The pattern for such a sentence is

Actor + Action → Goal
(Subject-Verb-Complement)

TRANSITIVE VERBS

The verb *hit* carries the action across from the subject to a complement. Because they receive the action, words used as this kind of complement are called **direct objects**.

The verb is called **transitive**, from the Latin root *trans-*, or across. A transitive verb carries the action from the subject *across* to the object. You find the same sense of *across* in other words, such as *transport*, *transfer*, and *transatlantic*.

INTRANSITIVE VERBS

Verbs that don't take objects are **intransitive**. The *in* means they do *not* carry action to a complement. Some verbs can be either transitive or intransitive, depending on their use in a sentence. Consider the following:

- The bonfire burned.
  Charley burned the bacon.
- Chipmunks play.
  The soloist played the viola.
- The bubble burst.
  The puppy burst the balloon.

LINKING VERBS

Consider the following subjects and verbs:

Lisa became _____?_____
The play seemed _____?_____
Andrew is _____?_____

Each lacks a word to complete its meaning. Each needs a complement.

Notice the kinds of words that fit the blank spaces and complete the meaning of each sentence.

Lisa = a scientist.
The play: long.
Andrew = brother.

None of these three complements receive the action of the verb. Instead, they either rename or describe the subject. Therefore, they are called **subjective complements**, and the verbs acting with them are called **linking verbs**.

Three Steps to Finding the Complement

1. Find the subject.
2. Find the verb, including any helpers.
3. Name the subject and verb; then ask *Who?* or *What?* The answer will be the complement, if the sentence has one.

Remember, there are three types of verbs.

1. Transitive verbs, which carry action across to a direct object/complement.
2. Intransitive verbs, which have no complement.
3. Linking verbs, which serve as a go-between for the subject and a related subjective complement.

PRACTICE

Find the subject/verb/complement (if any) in the following sentences.

1. First, find the subject. Ask *who* or *what* is the sentence about?
2. Next, find the verb. Name the subject, and ask, "Did what?"
3. Ask *Who?* or *What?* (after saying subject and verb together) to find a complement.

Example

After a few minutes, the woman beside me on the bus took a sandwich out of her handbag.

> Subject = (the) woman
> > (The) woman did *what?*   *Took.*
> Verb = took
> > (The) woman took *what?*   *sandwich.*
> Complement = (a) sandwich

Subject/Verb/Complement (S-V-C) = (The) woman/took/(a) sandwich.

1. Without wasting any time, Laird threw the crudely wrapped, ticking box into the river.
2. Fires in the western regions of the United States destroy many valuable forests every year.
3. The famous and talented artist exactly captured the expression of his subject.
4. The limousine from the airport will arrive at the hotel in forty minutes.
5. Each circus clown wears a funny disguise especially his own.

Answers

1. Laird threw the package.
2. Fires destroy forests.
3. The artist captured the expression.
4. The limousine will arrive.
5. The clown wears a disguise.

The rest of the words give you the details, but to understand grammar and to be a good reader, you should always be able to identify the main words of every sentence:

> Subject + Verb + Complement (if any)
> Actor / Action /   Goal

Chapter 7

Pronouns

He won a million dollars in the lottery.

How would you react if someone told you this? Chances are, what you'd want to know is "What person is *he?*" or "*Who* won the lottery?" You're really interested in a noun or a name—the subject, in fact.

Our boss just won a million dollars in the lottery.

"Did he?" You might reply. "I bet I could find better uses for it than he can."

Pronouns have a useful job in sentences: they take the place of nouns. Sometimes this purpose gets lost in grammar books, and sentences like the one beginning this chapter are given to show pronouns at work. But it's not a good example because there's no way to know what noun means the same as the pronoun *he.*

A **pronoun** is a word that serves as a "stand-in" for a noun. It saves a noun from being repeated too often and also works when the exact name is not known.

SPEAKING PERSONALLY

Personal pronouns are the pronouns we use most often. To illustrate how important they are, here's a scene showing what a job interview might be like if personal pronouns hadn't been invented. In the personnel office of a TV network, a young woman, Lori Lewis, enters and sits opposite the manager's desk.

INTERVIEWER: What is the name of the person applying for the job?

LORI LEWIS: The name is Lori Lewis.

INTERVIEWER: What kind of experience does Lori Lewis have?

LORI LEWIS: Lori Lewis has worked three years at a television station in Pittsburgh, Pennsylvania.

INTERVIEWER: What position did Lori Lewis hold there?

LORI LEWIS: The position was as an anchorperson. Would the Interviewer like to see Lori Lewis's video tapes?

INTERVIEWER: Where are the video tapes?

LORI LEWIS: Lori Lewis has the video tapes with Lori Lewis. Lori Lewis also has a letter of reference from Lori Lewis's superior, Marvin Mercer. Marvin Mercer is the station manager.

INTERVIEWER: Would Lori Lewis like the Interviewer to look at the tapes now?

Substitute personal pronouns for nouns in the above dialogue so that it sounds natural. Is there any doubt that we *need* personal pronouns?

HOW PRONOUNS EXPRESS PERSON AND NUMBER

Personal pronouns are easy to chart and worth keeping in your memory as an important language tool.

Grammar shows them to have three major categories:

- First Person
- Second Person
- Third Person

Each group has two subdivisions:

- Singular (one of each)
- Plural (two or more)

Like most parts of grammar, this organization fits the way people talk and think.

I'm Number One: The First Person

An individual sees the world through only one pair of eyes, and all of us see ourselves as Number One, or the **first person**. *I* know only what comes within my orbit. So the first person (singular) is always *I*. First person includes *me*, *mine*, and *myself*, along with *I*.

You're Number Two: The Second Person

When *I* am with someone else, that person becomes the **second person**, whom I think of and call *you*. The second person (singular) consists of *you* and its related forms, *yours* and *yourself*.

Everyone Else Is Number Three: The Third Person

The third person (singular) has a bit more to it. When *you* and *I* talk *about* someone or something else, we use the **third person singular** pronouns *he*, *she*, and *it*, along with their other forms.

- he (him, his, and himself)
- she (her, hers, and herself)
- it (it, its, and itself)

Plural Pronouns

Knowing the singular makes the plural easy.

First Person Plural
   I + you = we
        (us, ours, ourselves)
Second Person Plural
   you + you = you
        (you, yours, yourselves—like the singular, with one exception)
Third Person Plural
   two or more of he, she, or it = they
        (them, theirs, themselves)

(For a more detailed discussion of personal pronouns, see Chapter 16.)

Personal Pronouns that Take the Place of Noun Subjects

	Singular	*Plural*
First person	I	we
Second person	you	you
Third person	he, she, it	they

Agreement

A personal pronoun usually takes the place of the noun that it both agrees with and follows most closely. A pronoun must match its noun in *number* (singular or plural) and gender (whether *he*, *she*, or *it*). Of course, the pronoun *I* always means the person speaking, and the pronoun *You* means those spoken to.

In your reading, always check to make sure what noun a pronoun is replacing. This is one key to becoming a better reader.

When you write, make sure you don't confuse your reader about what noun a pronoun stands for.

Example

- I just used my pen to write a check, and now I can't find it.

Can't find the check or the pen?

- (better) I can't find my pen, even though I just used it to write a check.

PRACTICE

List the personal pronouns and the nouns they replace in the following sentences. Which sentence seems unclear? Why?

1. Jon felt that he must have made a mistake.
2. Jon told Barry that he must have made a mistake.
3. When Luke tells jokes, they never get laughs because he always confuses the punch line.
4. As the blizzard raged, it caused the people in the cabin to wonder if it could stand up against the storm and if they had enough food to last.

(For answers, see page 195.)

Understanding how pronouns work also helps in reading. As you read, you should always know what noun each pronoun replaces. As you read the following paragraphs (adapted from Graham Greene's *The Lawless Roads*), identify and list each personal pronoun. After it, write the noun it stands for.

Note: Label *I* as stand-in pronoun for *person speaking*. The pronoun *he* stands for three different nouns in the selection. Notice how *he* replaces the noun that comes before it and keeps that meaning until another noun having the sense of *he* is used.

THE PHILOSOPHER

The priest and I went up the stairs in a dingy building to find the old German teacher of languages who would come with me in case I needed an interpreter. Some years before he had lived with the General and tried to teach him German. There were always too many people waiting with petitions. Seldom fewer than sixty of them came a day. He never had any chance of a quiet time with the irregular verbs.

We beat on the door for a long while, until at last it was secretively opened by a young man. He wore a grubby dressing gown, was one-eyed and pockmarked. The flat was dusty and unaired. A few books lay about on the floor. There were a blackboard and some broken teacups. It was like a place temporarily put together by gypsies. The old professor had thin white hair, a long white moustache, and whitened, bony hands. He had an air of melancholy good breeding. He was very clean and very worn. He was like an old-fashioned vase standing among the junk at the end of an auction.

He was a philosopher, he managed to insist, while he haggled gently over the pesos he was to be paid.

(For answers, see page 195.)

Chapter 8

Adjectives: The First Add-On

Everyone interested in cars knows what it means to modify an engine.

In much the same way, adjectives and adverbs modify words. They don't change the basic meanings of the words they modify; they "soup words up" and highlight certain qualities of the words they modify.

HOW ADJECTIVES MODIFY

Adjective A Word Used to Modify or Describe a Noun or a Pronoun

Adjectives at Work

- The <u>young</u> kicker missed the goal.
- The <u>old</u> kicker missed the goal.
- The <u>tense</u> kicker missed the goal.
- The <u>cocky</u> kicker missed the goal.

Exactly the same thing happened in all four sentences, but a difference in adjectives makes us "see" a happening differently and react differently, too.

Big or little?
Green or yellow?
Friendly or fierce?
Five or fifty?

These are some of the differences that adjectives can make without changing the basic meanings of nouns or pronouns they describe.

HOW TO FIND AN ADJECTIVE

1. First, and always, know your way around the sentence. Find the subject/verb/complement (S-V-C) or subject/verb (S-V).
2. Identify all other words used as nouns or pronouns in the sentence.
3. Check for adjectives by determining whether they answer "*What* one?" about a noun or a pronoun.

Example #1

The new movie received good reviews.

   (S-V-C) (The) movie/received/reviews

   What movie? The *new* one.

   new is an adjective, modifying the noun subject, *movie*.

   What reviews? *Good* ones.

   good is an adjective, modifying the noun complement, *reviews*.

In English, most adjectives come before the nouns or pronouns they modify, but there are a few exceptions.

Example #2

The path, rough and narrow, challenged us.

   (S-V-C) (The) path/challenged/us

   Nouns/pronouns: path, us

   What path? The *rough* one. The *narrow* one.

   Both *rough* and *narrow* are adjectives, modifying the subject noun, *path*.

Of course, the sentence could just as easily have been written, "The rough and narrow path challenged us." However, adjectives are sometimes put after the noun for emphasis.

Example #3

The hiker carried a heavy knapsack.

   (S-C-V) (The) hiker/carried/knapsack.

   Nouns: hiker, knapsack

   What knapsack? A *heavy* one.

   Heavy is an adjective, modifying the noun direct object, *knapsack*.

You could also say, "The knapsack is heavy," or "It is heavy." In both cases, *heavy* is still an adjective, but it is now used as a subjective complement. It both completes the meaning of the sentence and modifies the subject. (*Question:* What kind of verb can use an adjective as a complement?)

ADJECTIVE OR NOUN?

Adjective is simply a label, given to describe the work a word does in a particular sentence. In English, the same word often can serve as a noun or adjective, depending on its use.

Example #4

The old car needs new tires.
  (S-V-C) (The) car/needs/tires.
  Nouns: car, tires
The car dealer offered a discount.
  (S-V-C) (The) dealer/offered/discount.
  Nouns: dealer, discount
    What dealer? The *car* dealer.

In the second sentence, *car* is used as an adjective, to modify the subject noun, *dealer.* In the first example, *car* is used as the noun subject, and has its own adjective, *old. Pearl* and *Florida* work the same two ways in the next pairs of sentences:

- The pearl was huge.
  The pearl necklace was a gift.
- Florida attracts tourists.
  Florida citrus growers dread frost.

Note: In the second sentence, both *Florida* and *citrus* are adjectives, modifying the noun, growers.

ADJECTIVES THAT LIMIT BY NUMBER

Example #5

Several critics panned the film.
Five weeks passed.
The winner received a million dollars.

It's clear that *several, five,* and *million* are adjectives in these sentences, but note their use in the following.

Several refused the invitation.
Five tried the product.
A million would cover the debt.

What is their use in the second set?

To find adjectives of number, some people ask "How many?" instead of "What one or ones?" Use the question that works best for you.

PRACTICE

Find the adjectives in the following selection from *The Ra Expeditions*, Thor Heyerdahl's account of his voyage across the Atlantic Ocean in a craft made of papyrus reeds. Before listing its adjectives, get to know your way around the selection by identifying nouns, pronouns, and verbs. Remember to check adjectives by asking, "*What (noun)?*" Some of Heyerdahl's sentences are more complex than you've worked with so far, so it may be a challenge to find all the adjectives Heyerdahl uses to describe a day when the sea was "full of life."

IN THE CLUTCHES OF THE SEA

Flying fish rained about us. Another moonfish drifted by, large and round and inert. Something invisible engulfed the hook on Georges' fixed fishing rod and made off with the whole line. Before he could pull it in, a hulking great fish swallowed the first, so Georges' catch was a severed fishhead. Meanwhile Ra *was skimming over the wave ridges at record speed, and we were all disappointed when Norman announced a moderate day's run after taking our noon position. We were being pulled south by a lateral current. In the last twenty-four hours the starboard corner of* Ra's *stern had sunk so far that the lower crossbeam of the steering gear was always dipping into the waves and acting as a brake. The water was permanently ankle-deep aft, and wavetops were constantly washing right up to the crate containing the life raft under the bridge. At every wave the crate shifted and chafed at the ropes holding the papyrus together.*

(For answers, see page 196.)

Chapter 9

Adverbs:
Add-On #2

Adverbs can show up almost anywhere in a sentence. Yet they have very specific work to do and very specific questions to answer.

AD + VERB

The word itself makes it easy to remember that an adverb modifies a verb, just as an adjective modifies a noun or pronoun. In addition, an adverb can also modify an *adjective* and even another *adverb*.

Like adjectives, adverbs answer definite questions about the words they describe. The best way to learn about adverbs is by observing them at work.

ADVERBS THAT MODIFY VERBS

What conclusions can you draw about adverbs that modify verbs, on the basis of those underlined here?

- Kit walked slowly.
- The child timidly asked permission.
- They always arrive early.
- Early settlers determinedly headed west.
- The angry boy broke the window purposely.

Conclusions

1. Many adverbs seem to end in -ly.
2. They often have an adjective base, as in

slow	slowly
timid	timidly
determined	determinedly

3. Some -ly words, such as *early*, can be used as adjectives or adverbs without a change in form.

4. Adverbs that modify verbs answer some very specific questions: When? Where? Why? How?

- walked *How?*   slowly
- asked *How?*   timidly
- arrive *When?*   early
    How often?   always
- headed *How?*   determinedly
    Where?   west
- broke *Why?*   purposely
    (or *How?*)

Note: *How, where,* and *why* often work as adverbs themselves. They are especially handy in asking questions.

Adverbs that Answer *When?*

then	always
now	never
sometimes	soon
often	afterward
rarely	beforehand

Adverbs that Answer *Where?*

here	there
near	far
away	close

Adverbs that Answer *How?*

sweetly	bitterly
honestly	slyly
cheerfully	sadly
brightly	dully
carefully	hopefully

Adverbs that Answer *Why?* or *How?*

purposely	accidentally
hurtfully	helpfully

Naturally, you could list many other adverbs, too. How? Additionally, or *too*. *Too* is thus an adverb. *Also* is an adverb, also.

HOW WORDS WORK

To find the right answer, just ask the right question.

Since a word can work in more than one way, its use depends on the sentence. It's sometimes tricky to identify adverbs that we usually think of as nouns or adjectives. In the following pairs of sentences, see how the underlined words first answer "what?" as nouns, then answer adverb questions as adverbial nouns.

- <u>Monday</u> begins the week.
  I begin work <u>Monday</u>.
- <u>Tomorrow</u> holds a promise.
  The team arrives <u>tomorrow</u>.
- A <u>home</u> becomes a haven.
  He hurried <u>home</u>.

For adverbs, position in a sentence does not necessarily determine which word(s) they're modifying.

- The rich man has <u>always</u> donated <u>generously</u> to worthwhile charities.
- The rich man <u>always</u> has donated <u>generously</u> . . .
- <u>Always</u>, the rich man has <u>generously</u> donated . . .
- The rich man has donated <u>generously</u> <u>always</u> . . .

Have you found the S-V in the previous sentences?

S-V: (The) man/has donated

Notice how the adverb sometimes comes between the verb and its helpers. Always be sure to find the entire verb string.

ADVERBS THAT MODIFY ADJECTIVES

How Big Was He?

- He was *so* big.
- He was *very* big.
- He was *rather* big.
- He was *extremely* big.

- He was *not* big.
- He was *really* big.
- He was *terribly* big.
- He was *too* big.

And that's how adverbs modify adjectives.

A Word about Being Right

Here's another point where knowing how grammar works can help you understand problems with English. Again and again, you hear sportscasters and coaches comment, "Brodhause is a real great player. He played a real fine game. We look forward to a real good season." How are they using *real*? The real answer is "incorrectly." How great? How fine? How good? In each case *real*, the adjective form, is being asked to modify another adjective and do the work of an adverb. It really should be *really*.

Can someone be pretty tall? According to the formation of adverbs and adjectives, someone can be both pretty and tall, but not pretty tall.

> The picture is pretty.
> The Southern belle smiled prettily.

Can someone be prettily tall? Never! Careful speakers and writers think of *pretty* as an adjective or verb that means to be or make *pleasing* or *attractive*.

It's too bad, but there are no "correct" adverbs that have the exact meaning of *sorta*, *kinda*, *a little*, and *pretty*. Both *sorta* and *kinda* actually consist of two words: *sort of* and *kind of*. Here they are in accepted uses:

- I like that *kind* of car.
- Pierce is a trustworthy *sort* of man.

In both examples, *kind* and *sort* are nouns that mean variety or class. *Little* and *pretty* are usually adjectives. Only words such as *quite*, *rather*, and *somewhat*, all "real" adverbs, are really "right" in their place.

ADVERBS THAT MODIFY ADVERBS

- The package came *too* late. *How* late?
- The police handled the bomb *very* carefully. *How* carefully?

Most adverbs are easy to identify. Whether they modify verbs, adjectives, or other adverbs, they answer the adverb questions: When? Where? Why? and How?

Not *Is Important*

- The message has come.
  Chris has taken the examination.
- The message has not come.
  Chris has not taken the examination.

The little word *not* completely changes the meaning of the second set of sentences. Yet it doesn't change their S-V-C.

(S-V) (The) message/has come
(S-V-C) Chris/has taken/examination

To make a verb negative in the present and past tenses, a verb and the adverb *not* act together in a special way. Notice how helping verbs are necessary when a verb takes a negative turn.

a. Most adults read. Some adults do not read.
   Some adults don't read.
   Some adults can not read.
   Some adults can't read.
b. Kim likes rock. Kim does not like rock.
   Kim doesn't like rock.
c. Dan went early. Dan did not go early.
   Dan didn't go early.

Note: The past tense of the verb (he *went*; she *called*) does not take a helper. Therefore, when *not* is used, the helping verb expresses the past tense and combines with the first part of the verb (he *did* not *go*; she *did* not *call*).

Neither the adverb *not* nor its contracted form *n't* should be included in the (S-V-C) string.

a. (S-V) adults/read; adults/do read; adults/do read; adults/can read; adults/can read
b. (S-V-C) Kim/likes/rock; Kim/does like/rock; Kim/does like/rock
c. (S-V) Dan/went; Dan/did go; Dan/did go

Of course, helping verbs can also be used to give emphasis to the positive sense of the verb.

- Willy does try hard.

PRACTICE

Good writers use strong, precise nouns and verbs in their writing. These solid parts of language carry meaning best. In the following excerpt from *The Nightmare Years 1930–1940*, Vol. 2, of *20th Century Journey*, see how William L. Shirer uses a straightforward, journalistic style. Be aware of the powering nouns and verbs. Never forget the importance of the S-V-C.

Careless use of modifiers weakens writing. As you list the adverbs in the passage, notice how every one of Shirer's adjectives and adverbs is important to the account.

WAR SEEMS AT HAND

The Czechs frantically called up one class of reserves and put their great fortress line on alert. I hurried up to Prague.

It looked there as if war was at hand. The cabinet met. The General Staff met. Conflicting intelligence poured in from the various capitals. Rumors were rife. Hastily called-up reserve troops embarked for the "front." I tried frantically to get the Czechs to put their new shortwave transmitter into action [and let us] broadcast directly to New York. The Germans refused us telephone lines through Germany, the only lines we could hook up with transmitters in Geneva or London.

(For answers, see page 196.)

Chapter 10

Prepositions:
Relating One Word
to Another

CAN WE GET ALONG WITHOUT PREPOSITIONS?

Yes, but not very well.

- The woman is the manager.

> What woman?
> > She is wearing a beige jacket.
> What does she manage?
> > She manages the bank.

- The woman <u>in</u> the beige jacket is manager <u>of</u> the bank.

In the sentence above, the preposition *in* shows the relationship between *woman* and *jacket*, and the preposition *of* relates *manager* to *bank*. There are other ways to combine ideas, but using prepositions is often the clearest, handiest, and most direct way.

PREPOSITIONS IN ACTION

- The woman <u>in</u> the beige *jacket* is manager <u>of</u> the *bank*.

Here is how to check a preposition, using *in* as an example. Ask "*In* what?" or "*In* whom?"—the questions that find nouns and pronouns. The answer, in this case *jacket*, is called the **object of the preposition**. It will always be a noun or pronoun. Taken together, all the words from the preposition to its object constitute a **prepositional phrase**. Here it's *in the beige jacket*.

What does the preposition *in* do? It puts the jacket on the woman, which is a very useful task for a part of speech to perform. Prepositions help to clarify relationships with a minimum of words.

> A preposition relates
> its noun or pronoun object
> to another word
> in the sentence.

The word "preposition" itself helps explain how it works. *Pre*-indicates that it comes *before* a noun or pronoun, called its object. Its purpose is to show the place (or *position*) of its object in relation to some other word. See Figure 10-1 for an illustration of the relationships indicated by some frequently used prepositions.

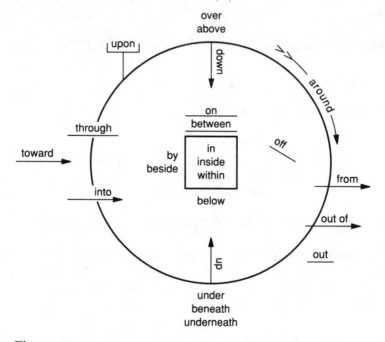

Figure 10-1

To discover how prepositions work, experiment with those given in Figure 10-1. Vary a sentence by using different prepositions to fill in the blank space, and see how they change the meaning.

Draw a line _____ the geometrical figures.

Among the possibilities are

Draw a line <u>above</u> the geometrical figures.
Draw a line <u>inside</u> the geometrical figures.

Examples

The cat hid <u>under</u> the bed.
Guards kept watch <u>around</u> the clock.
<u>Inside</u> the hollow tree trunk, a hunter found the stolen money.
<u>Through</u> the open window we could feel a fresh breeze.

And Even More Prepositions

The man/
    <u>with</u> brown eyes
    <u>in</u> the photo
    <u>from</u> Dallas
    <u>of</u> her dreams
    <u>at</u> the door
    <u>aboard</u> ship
    <u>without</u> shoes
    <u>behind</u> the fence
        . . . is Harry!

Prepositions make the connection.

To Identify Prepositions in Sentences

- First, check the subject-verb-complement. Neither subject nor complement will be an object of a preposition.
- Spot possible prepositions, and ask "Whom?" or "What?" after each.
- Every preposition will have a noun or pronoun object included in its prepositional phrase.

Note: Some prepositions consist of more than one word.

because of
according to
in spite of
instead of
as of

PREPOSITIONAL PHRASES AS ADJECTIVES

The young man with brown eyes is Harry.
    What man?
        a. the <u>young</u> one
        b. the one <u>with brown eyes</u>

The entire prepositional phrase, *with brown eyes*, works as an adjective to modify the noun, man, just as the one-word adjective, *young*, does.

This illustrates one of the most important principles in grammar. A word can function by itself in a sentence, but it can also become part of a **phrase**, a group of two or more grammatically related words. Acting as a unit, the phrase also works as a single part of speech in a sentence. In this way grammar is not very different from any other mechanical device. For example, a bolt can connect one piece to another. Then it becomes a part of a unit, which has a special function of its own to perform.

Example

- One of my favorite books by Thor Heyerdahl describes his voyage across the Pacific.

  (S-V-C) One/describes/voyage

  What One?   *of my favorite books*

  What books?   *by Thor Heyerdahl*

  What voyage?   *across the Pacific*

As you can see, a prepositional phrase, *by Thor Heyerdahl*, modifies a noun, *books*, which is itself an object in the prepositional phrase before it.

Adjective prepositional phrases usually follow the noun or pronoun they modify.

- The book by Thor Heyerdahl about his Pacific adventure has the title of *Kon-Tiki.*

  What book?   *by Thor Heyerdahl*

  What Thor Heyerdahl?   *about his Pacif*...STOP!

    That doesn't make sense!

  What book?   *about his Pacific adventure*

    That's it!

  What title?   *of Kon-Tiki*

PRACTICE

Identify the prepositional phrases, along with the nouns and pronouns they modify. It may help to spot each S-V-C first.

1. The best scene in the movie was one near the beginning with loads of laughs.
2. The shrill call of the alarm clock disturbed my dream about a life of leisure in Tahiti.
3. *A gaggle of geese* is the term for a group of these fowl creatures.
4. The sign upon the post gave a warning about the dangerous condition of the old bridge.
5. A gleam of light through the farmhouse windows renewed the hope of the tired man.

(For answers, see page 196.)

PREPOSITIONAL PHRASES AS ADVERBS

Like other adverbs, prepositional phrases can modify verbs as well as adjectives and other adverbs.

- Many Northerners go to Florida during the winter.
    Go *where*?   *to Florida*
    Go *when*?   *during the winter*

Both prepositional phrases work as adverbs, modifying the verb *go*. As adverbs, prepositional phrases answer the same questions as any other adverb: *When*? *Where*? *Why*? *How*?

PRACTICE

The five sentences that follow contain twelve prepositional phrases used as adverbs. Identify them and the verbs, adjectives, or adverbs they modify.

1. Until this year José worked for a Tucson newspaper.
2. After the game all the people rushed out of the stadium toward their cars.
3. Airline passengers can put luggage in the plane's belly, under their seats, or in overhead compartments.
4. People young at heart sometimes succeed because of their optimistic attitudes.
5. The ransom note was written by hand in an almost illegible scrawl.

(For answers, see page 196.)

SOME ADVICE ABOUT USAGE

Here's an old saying, taught to generations of grammar students: "Never end a sentence with a preposition." (Or, to break the rule, "Never use a preposition to end a sentence with.") This is a rule more firmly based in Latin grammar than English. Yet, when you know how prepositional phrases work, you can understand why some people remember the old rule and still feel annoyed upon hearing a preposition that is separated from its object. Even though it's natural in English to ask, "What are you waiting for?" the careful speaker or writer will also know the formal usage:

- At what time will you come?
- For whom were you looking?
  rather than
- What time will you come at?
- Who were you looking for?

It is more important to avoid expressions such as these:

- Where are you going to?
- When is it at?
- Where is it at?

In all three questions, the final words have no work at all to do, since *where* means "to or at what place," and *when* means "at what time." Simply say

- Where are you going?
- When is it?
- Where is it?

WHEN IS A "PREPOSITION" NOT A PREPOSITION?

Remember, a word's use in a sentence determines its part of speech.

- Baxter went <u>around</u> the world.
  The car spun <u>around</u>.
- Our candidate came <u>through</u>.
  Karen worked her way <u>through</u> college.
- After the rain, the game went <u>on</u>.
  The debate took place <u>on</u> television.
  Ward turned <u>on</u> the television.

Which of the underlined words are prepositions and which are adverbs? Only the last sentence should be a problem. (What is the S-V-C?) If "on the television" is a prepositional phrase, what does it modify?

- Ward turned the television <u>on</u>.

A change of word order makes it easier to see that *on* is actually an adverb.

- Ms. Tyler came <u>in</u>. She sat <u>down</u>. She looked <u>up</u>.

In each of these examples, the final word is an adverb, not a preposition. Remember that a preposition *always* has an object. Together, they form a phrase that clarifies the relationship of one word to another in a sentence.

PRACTICE

The following selection comes from *Cry of the Kalahari* by Mark and Delia Owens, an American couple who spent seven years studying animal life in Africa's Kalahari desert.

First read the passage to discover what it feels like to be in a desert afire. Then reread it to identify the prepositional phrases and the words they modify. Be on the lookout for adverbs, too. *Note:* Be sure to choose the right object; sometimes words often used as nouns are working as adjectives.

EARLY IN THEIR STAY, A FIRE ENGULFS THEIR CAMP

The morning wore on, the winds blew harder, and the roar from the fire grew louder. More and more ash rained into camp and swirled across the ground in the churning air. By midafternoon, driven by the heavy desert winds, the first flame reached the top of East Dune. It paused for a moment, licking at the tall grasses and lower branches of a tree, then leaped quickly to the top, turning the tree into a thirty-foot torch. Another flame crested the dune, then another. A line of fire invaded the woodlands, and whole trees exploded like flares.

The intense heat created its own wind, a wind that fed oxygen to the flames and spurred them down the duneslopes toward the riverbed at an incredible speed, sweeping them through grass and bush as far north and south as we could see. Nothing could have prepared us for that sight.

. . . After the fire passed us it marched on across the dune tops into the Kalahari, lighting the night sky like a spectacular sunset. Behind it, the cool pink glow of burned-out trees and logs remained, until the fire's crimson was lost in the blush of dawn.

Did you notice how nouns and verbs power the selection, to keep the excitement going, while prepositional phrases answer other questions?

(For answers, see page 196.)

Chapter 11

Coordinating Conjunctions: One and One Make Two

Conjunctions Connect

con = with

junction = the place where two things join or meet

So a conjunction is simply a word used to join or connect words, phrases, clauses, or sentences.

AND: THE MOST COMMON CONJUNCTION

If you can understand the way the word *and* works in a sentence, you'll find it easy to understand how all of the other conjunctions work, too.

And is one of a group called the **coordinating conjunctions**, which connect two equal things.

Connecting Two Equal Words

- Lions and tigers are native to different continents.
- Dina speaks and reads Spanish.
- The small and agile girl is a remarkable gymnast.
- The flag waved to and fro in the breeze.

Have you identified the parts of speech that *and* joins in the examples above? Now check the following.

- Paul and you are alike in some ways.

Although *Paul* is a noun and *you* a pronoun, in this sentence both are equal. Why? Both are subjects of the sentence.

Parts of a Sentence Joined by Coordinating Conjunctions Are Called Compound

Sentences may have compound subjects, compound verbs, compound objects of a preposition, and so on. For example: Minerva and Athena are both names for the goddess of wisdom.

$$
\begin{array}{cc}
& \text{Minerva} \\
\text{(S-V-C)} \quad \text{and} & \text{/are/names} \\
& \text{Athena}
\end{array}
$$

Minerva–Athena is the compound subject.

Connecting Two Equal Phrases

- Ann searched in the drawer and under the bed.
- You can enter and might win.
- We will go and return on the same day. (Note: Will serves as a helper for both underlined words.)
- Some people get an idea in their heads and will not let it go.

In the last sentence, *and* joins two complete predicates. A **complete predicate** is a verb plus its complement and all of its modifiers.

   Caution: Of course, "and" shouldn't be asked to join words that are being put to different uses in a sentence.

> **Example:** I went shopping and then to a restaurant. ("Shopping" and "to a restaurant" aren't equal.)
>
> **Better:** I went to the mall and then to a restaurant.
> I shopped at the mall and then went to a restaurant.

Connecting Two Sentences or Clauses

- You have done the job well, and I congratulate you.
- "We have met the enemy, and they are ours."

A Sentence + A Sentence = A Compound Sentence

- You have done the job well.
    (S-V-C) You/have done/(the) job
- I congratulate you.
    (S-V-C) I/congratulate/you

Each of these is a **simple sentence** because each has just one S-V-C. Each can also be called an **independent clause**, because it can stand alone as a sentence. When two independent clauses are joined in one sentence, that sentence is called a **compound sentence**.

- You have done the job well, and I congratulate you.

Two or more independent clauses may be joined with *and* or another coordinating conjunction. Sometimes the conjunction is omitted, and a semicolon is used instead.

Note: A *clause* is any group of words having a subject and verb.

COMPOUND SENTENCES, COMPOUND PARTS

1. Simple sentence with a compound subject.

The brakes and clutch need adjustment.

(S-V-C) (The) $\begin{Bmatrix} \text{brakes} \\ \text{(and)} \\ \text{clutch} \end{Bmatrix}$ /need/adjustment

2. Simple sentence with a compound predicate.

Jake left early and missed the excitement.
(S-V-C) Jake/left
        (and)
        missed/(the) excitement

3. Compound sentence.

His victory took courage, and it also required skill.
(S-V-C) Victory/took/courage
        (and)
(S-V-C) it/required/skill

Of course, the possibilities are endless. What about a compound sentence with independent clauses that have their own compound parts? Work on it!

HOW TO BE SURE WHAT *AND* JOINS

First, check what follows the conjunction. Then, look in front of it until you find the part—words, phrases, or clauses—that matches something after the conjunction.

- You can try the product and decide for yourself.

Since *decide* is a verb form, you must look for a verb form before *and*. That's *try* (don't include *can*, which is a helper for both).

And is like a link in a chain. It connects directly to what's next to it. Since it joins equal things, you must check both ways until you find two equal parts: words, phrases or clauses that work alike.

In the example, all the words from *try* to *and* must be included; *and* joins try the product to decide for yourself. In the next examples, *and* joins the parts underlined. Can you explain why? What is the work of the underlined parts?

- The family traveled to Nevada and California during their vacation.
- They camped in several national parks and near the ocean.

Knowing what *and* joins helps you sort out ideas. It leads to a better understanding of how words and ideas work together as parts of a whole.

COMPOUND PARTS IN A SERIES

- The store carries athletic gear and exercise equipment and sportswear.

You do not need an *and* to separate every item in a series of words, phrases, or clauses. *Put a comma in the place of all but the final one.*

- The store carries athletic gear, exercise equipment, and sportswear.
- Deer, rabbits, squirrels, pheasants, foxes, bears, buffaloes, and eagles were once plentiful in the American wilderness.
- Brad studied, Betsy watched television, and she got the A on the test.

Caution: In using *and*, be sure it's clear what you're doing.

- I'm bringing Bill, Bob, and Ben, and Bruce will bring Bert.

At times it's better to use two simple sentences.

PRACTICE

Using *and* is the first way most of us discover to connect ideas and sentences. Sometimes young and beginning writers overuse *and*s or put them together in a confusing way. Yet the knowledgeable writer can use the same word for telling effects.

In the following passages, notice how Zora Neale Hurston, in her novel *Their Eyes Were Watching God*, uses language effectively to portray the feelings of a simple folk. Here, Hurston describes the coming of a storm on Lake Okeechobee in Florida.

A MONSTER AWAKENS

It was hot and sultry and Janie left the field and went home.

. . . That night the palm and banana trees began that long distance talk with rain. Several people took fright and picked up and went in to Palm Beach anyway. A thousand buzzards held a flying meet and then went above the clouds and stayed.

. . . Several men collected at Tea Cake's house and sat around stuffing courage into each other's ears. Janie baked a big pan of beans and something she called sweet biscuits and they all managed to be happy enough.

. . . Sometime that night the winds came back. Everything in the world had a strong rattle, sharp and short like Stew Beef vibrating the drum head near the edge with his fingers. By morning Gabriel was playing the deep tones in the center of the drum. So when Janie looked out of her door she saw the drifting mists gathered in the west—that cloud field of the sky—to arm themselves with thunders and march forth against the world. Louder and higher and lower and wider the sound and motion spread, mounting, sinking, darking.

It woke up old Okeechobee and the monster began to roll in his bed. Began to roll and complain like a peevish world on a grumble. The folk in the quarters and the people in the big houses further around the shore heard the big lake and wondered. The people felt uncomfortable but safe because there were the seawalls to chain the senseless monster in his bed. The folks let the people do the thinking. If the castles thought themselves secure, the cabins needn't worry. Their decision was already made as always. Chink up your cracks, shiver in your wet beds and wait on the mercy of the Lord.

Notice how Hurston's use of *and* gives the selection movement by making all of the ideas relatively equal. Ernest Hemingway is another novelist who uses the word *and* for a similar effect in his work.

Even though Hurston chooses to write in simple language, she uses both precise words and colorful expression. What are some examples?

Sometimes Hurston omits the subject of her sentence. Did you notice any examples? What effect did she seek by doing this?

To use language well, you must know how something works, not only to fix it, but also to know how to break the rules effectively.

MORE COORDINATING CONJUNCTIONS

You should remember six coordinating conjunctions.

      Set A: and   or   nor
      Set B: but   for   yet

All are short; their work in a sentence is not to call attention to themselves but to join two equal parts. (Sometimes, as in a series, they can even be replaced by a mere comma!)

Set A

- You can choose from blue or red.
- Would you prefer to live on a ranch or in a city apartment?
- I may go, or I may not.
- I have neither time nor money to waste.
- We had not slept, nor had we eaten.

Set B

But, *for*, and *yet*, when used as coordinating conjunctions, usually join independent clauses (or sentences). They are just as often seen as other parts of speech.

- Elliot's lottery winnings totaled six million dollars, but he kept working.
  Everyone but Claire has sent an answer.
- Jay missed the train, for he was stuck in a traffic jam.
  I left a message for you on the answering machine.
- The deal seems promising, yet I would like more details about it.
  The plane hasn't landed yet.

Note that *but*, *for*, and *yet* work as prepositions or adverbs in the second sentence of each pair.

As a conjunction, each gives a clue about what to expect in the independent clause that follows.

> but: on the other hand
> for: seeing that (introducing an explanation)
> yet: nevertheless; however

PAIRED CONJUNCTIONS

- both/and
- not only/but also
- either/or
- neither/nor
- whether/or

Some conjunctions have a partner to signal what's coming and to emphasize their meaning. The five pairs are called **correlative conjunctions**.

Did you notice their use in comments about the selection by Zora Neale Hurston? If not, check to see them in action.

The first word of a correlative pair should come just before what is being joined.

> **Right:** The caller seemed <u>both</u> confused <u>and</u> upset.
> **Wrong:** The caller <u>both</u> seemed confused <u>and</u> upset.

In these examples, *and* is used to join the adjectives *confused* and *upset*; therefore, *both* should be placed immediately before the first adjective of the pair.

Compare the following:

> **Right:** The travel agent will both book your flight and make your hotel reservations.
> **Wrong:** The travel agent both will book your flight and make your hotel reservations.

The difference may seem small, but it's one that marks someone who "knows."

PRACTICE

Simple Sentences with Compound Parts

In the following sentences, pick out the conjunctions and the words they are joining. Identify the subject/verb/complements, remembering some will be compound.

1. The strong wind and driving rain made walking difficult.
2. Keith mislaid his billfold but found it in his car.
3. Both Beth and her parents were excited about her appointment to West Point.
4. You could neither hear nor see well from the back of the room.
5. The moon and the stars glowed and gleamed like seed pearls against the night sky.

Compound Sentences

Consider the conjunction in parentheses. Then, from the second column, match the simple sentence/independent clause that fits with the one in column 1.

1. I know the answer, (for)
2. You must come early, (or)
3. The experiment was a success, (but)
4. Jeff tried to look serious, (for)
5. I had never seen them before, (nor)
6. They were not expecting visitors, (but)
7. We were ahead by two touchdowns, (and)
8. We were ahead by two touchdowns, (but)

a. They tried not to look upset.
b. It will be hard to duplicate.
c. There was still a quarter to go.
d. I studied three hours.
e. Did I hope to see them again.
f. You might not find a seat.
g. We felt very confident.
h. His boss did not look in the mood for humor.

(For answers, see page 197.)

A NOTE ABOUT PUNCTUATION

Correct punctuation helps a reader understand the use of words more quickly and easily.

1. When coordinating conjunctions join just two words or phrases, no comma is used.

   - Blue and yellow are primary colors that combine to make green.
   - I plan to be in the office and at work by eight.

2. Use commas to separate items in a series.

   - Arizona, New Mexico, and Texas evoke images of the Old West.

3. Punctuate compound sentences by using a comma before the conjunction.

   - The idea sounds strange, but it just might work.

   With closely related clauses, compound sentences can sometimes be formed without the use of a conjunction; a semicolon takes the place of the comma and conjunction.

   - The curtain supposedly rose at eight. The play began an hour late.
   - The curtain supposedly rose at eight, but the play began an hour late.
   - The curtain supposedly rose at eight; the play began an hour late.

   Note: Use a semicolon to join two independent clauses that aren't connected by a coordinating conjunction, unless the clauses are short and closely related.

   - I came, I saw, I conquered.

The Eight Parts of Speech

Now that you have met seven of the eight parts of speech informally and seen how they work, here they are in their formal definitions. By now, of course, you should have an understanding that goes beyond the flat statements that follow.

1. **Noun:** any of a class of words naming or denoting a person, place, thing, idea, quality, etc.

2. **Verb:** any of a class of words expressing action, existence, or occurrence; any phrase or construction used as a verb.

3. **Pronoun:** a word used in the place of or as a substitute for a noun.

4. **Adjective:** any of a class of words used to limit or qualify a noun or *substantive* (a word or group of words "subbing" as a noun).

5. **Adverb:** any of a class of words used to modify the meaning of a verb, adjective, or other adverb, in regard to time, place, manner, means, cause, degree, etc. (*Note:* Do you recognize the adverb questions?)

6. **Preposition:** a relational word that connects a noun, pronoun, or noun phrase to another element of the sentence, such as a verb, a noun, or an adjective.

7. **Conjunction:** a word used to connect words, phrases, clauses, or sentences.

8. **Interjection:** Wow! Phew! A word expressing emotion or simple exclamation, thrown into a sentence without grammatical connection.

PART II

ACTION AND INTERACTION: THE SYSTEM AT WORK

Chapter 12

Word Order
Is Part of Meaning

In Modern English, [the relationships of words] are expressed through the device of fixed word order, our principal and indispensable grammatical device.

Webster's New World Dictionary, 1966

His the chased puppy tail.
The puppy chased his tail.
His tail chased the puppy.

Anyone who understands English knows that the middle sentence is the "normal" one. The last is silly. The first is a nonsensical jumble. The three examples stand as proof that English is, at its heart, a word order language.

SUBJECTS NATURALLY COME FIRST

The normal order of the English sentence is subject/verb/complement (or subject/verb). That's why a difficult sentence becomes easier to understand if you stop and identify these key words.

Unlike English, some languages use endings or inflections at the ends of words to show their use in a sentence. They might add -*um* to indicate a complement. In that way, the following sentences would be equally easy to understand.

The puppy chased hisum tailum.
Hisum tailum chased the puppy.

Ancient Latin and Greek use such inflections to signal how a word works in a sentence. English most often uses word order (or **syntax**).

At one time, many in the upper classes considered Latin and Greek far superior to English, which was low-class and vulgar. To give English higher status, some scholars tried to make its grammar mimic the grammars of Latin and Greek. It doesn't, of course, but we are still paying the price of that snobbery today. Even now, many grammars don't mention the importance of word order to an understanding of how English works.

The **natural order** of an English sentence is as follows:

Mr. Anderson plodded wearily up the stairs.
(S-V) Mr. Anderson/plodded

There you see it, a perfectly ordinary sentence. You see the subject first; you see what "it" is doing; finally an adverb and prepositional phrase tell you how and where.

Remember, one of the important tasks of language is to create an image in someone's mind. Early forms of written languages even used pictograms to transmit such images.

Is this the same sentence as the example above?

■ Up the stairs plodded Mr. Anderson wearily.
   (S-V) Mr. Anderson/plodded

Of course, it's clearly the same sentence, but it is possible to reverse the order to give you an image of the stairs first. Then you see Mr. Anderson plodding up them wearily. Don't the stairs seem longer this way?

This is called the transposed order. It means to take the S-V-C *across*, out of its natural order. In the **transposed order**, the verb or part of the predicate comes before the subject.

When writing sentences, avoid using the transposed order just to be different. You might end up confusing someone. You wouldn't want anyone to imagine a tail was chasing a puppy!

JUDGING SENTENCES BY PURPOSE

Sentences have four different categories, according to the purpose they are meant to achieve. The use of natural or transposed order has much to do with whether we send and receive the message clearly.

Statements

Statements are sentences that state, declare, or make known ideas, opinions, or other pieces of information. Most sentences are statements, and most statements are in natural order.

Examples

John likes pizza.
(S-V-C) John/likes/pizza

My uncle's car had run out of gas.
One of Roy's main problems has always been his laziness.
In my opinion Chris should have been promoted instead of Josh.
Marty might not remember to bring the tapes.

Commands

Commands are sentences that give direct orders to whomever they address. The subject, which is *always* "you," is *never* included in the clause.

Since the subject "you" is understood to come first, you can consider commands to have a natural order.

Examples

Shut the door.
(S-V-C) [You]/shut/(the) door
Do come to the ceremony.
(S-V) [You]/do come

Practice your lines for tomorrow's rehearsal.
Try to practice good manners in all your dealings.
Make a habit of being on time.
Remember the importance of syntax to English.

Questions

Questions are sentences that ask for an opinion, information, or another sort of response. Part or all of the verb is usually transposed to a position before the subject. How questions work will be discussed in detail later.

Examples

Did you hear him?
(S-V-C) You/did hear/him

Can you understand his point of view?
How much did that sweater cost?
What has Edie heard about the new project?
Did Fred appear nervous as the emcee?

Exclamations

Exclamations are sentences that express strong emotion or feeling. To call attention to this, exclamations often start with *How* or *What*, and also have the complement before the subject/verb. All exclamations should end in exclamation points.

Examples

How happy we were!
(S-V-C) We/were/happy

What a wonderful time we had!
How frightening the old house seemed with the wind rattling the shutters!
How clever you are!
What a difference your advice made!

PRACTICE

Decide whether the following are statements, questions, commands, or exclamations. It will be easier if you identify the S-V-C or S-V.

1. You will find the index at the end of a book.
2. How many people will be affected by the law?
3. Give consideration to other people's feelings.
4. After a long wait we were finally permitted inside the concert hall.
5. How surprised Kay looked about the news!
6. What excitement the announcement caused!
7. What do you think of the new boss?
8. Mail your entry in before July 31.

(For answers, see page 197.)

Formal Terminology for the Four Purposes of a Sentence

1. statement = **declarative sentence**
   A statement states or declares a fact.
   The Declaration of Independence makes declarative statements about the Colonists' intentions.

2. command = **imperative sentence**
   "Do as I say," he said imperatively.
3. question = **interrogative sentence**
   Has the lawyer finished his interrogation of the witness?
4. exclamation = **exclamatory sentence**
   "How obvious that is!" she exclaimed.

CHANGING WORD ORDER CHANGES PURPOSE

There are four basic ways of turning a statement into a question in English. Three of them require transposing part of the subject-verb-complement.

1. To signal a question, put part or all of the verb before the subject.

Statements
   a. Mike is going to California.
   b. He has been there before.
   c. Everyone was surprised by the verdict.

Questions
   a. Is Mike going to California?
   b. Has he been there before?
   c. Was everyone surprised by the verdict?

2. Add a helping verb before the subject to form a question.

Statements
   a. Fran speaks Chinese fluently.
   b. Kermit likes listening to jazz.
   c. Many people came to the exhibit.

Questions
   a. Can Fran speak Chinese fluently?
   b. Does Kermit like listening to jazz?
   c. Did many people come to the exhibit?

3. Use an adverb question as an opening word: *where, when, why,* or *how.*

Statements
   a. Charlene works at the zoo.
   b. She finishes work at 5 P.M.

c. I called the dentist for an appointment.

d. Wyman made the journey by dogsled.

Questions

a. Where does Charlene work?

b. When does she finish work?

c. Why did you call the dentist?

d. How did Wyman make the journey?

Note that the form of the question determines the answer. You could also ask, "Does Charlene work at the zoo?" Also, notice how some sentences add a helping verb as another sign of a question. Pronouns may change, too: "How are you?" becomes "I am fine."

4. *What? Who? Which?* also introduce questions.

Statements

a. Robert Redford directed the film.

b. I bought a new pair of skis.

c. The letter held welcome news.

d. The photographer printed the third pose.

e. Hank chose the convertible instead of the hardtop.

Questions

a. Who directed the film?

   (S-V-C) Who/directed/film

b. What did you buy?

   (S-V-C) you/did buy/what

c. What news did the letter hold?

   (S-V-C) letter/did hold/news

d. Which pose did the photographer print?

   (S-V-C) photographer/did print/pose

e. Which of the two cars did Hank choose?

   (S-V-C) Hank/did choose/which

From the S-V-C, you can see that in examples a, b, and e, *who, what,* and *which* are used as pronouns. *What* in c and *which* in d are adjectives.

One More Way to Be "Right"

The call was from the CEO.
From whom was the call?

The pronoun *who*—like the pronouns *he, she, I, we,* and *they*—has another form meant to work as an object of a verb or preposition.

It's one of the few ways English is still an inflected language, and it's becoming lost, too. Still, the careful speaker would say, "I don't know whom to thank," and "Whom did you ask?"

(For a further discussion of this concept, see p. 134.)

PRACTICE

Rewrite each of the following as a question, using one of the changes in word order that signal a question. More than one way is possible for several.

1. Chris has forgotten his promise.
2. You can understand his point of view.
3. Bonnie will be home tomorrow.
4. The car repairs cost over $200.
5. Sarah chose the less expensive car.
6. The magician was clever.

(For answers, see page 197.)

Make up an answer to the following questions. Remember, a question asked with *you*, requires *I* or *we* in its response. (You need not include *yes* or *no*.) Notice the S-V-C of each question and then write the answer in natural order.

1. Did your uncle's car run out of gas?
2. When do you expect the answer?
3. What kind of music does Wendy like?
4. Is the bargain a good one?
5. Have there been any calls for me?
6. Which kind of soft drink do you prefer, diet or regular?

Chapter 13

Just Enough Punctuation

A pause, a raising or lowering of the voice, an emphasis, perhaps a bit of body language: These are some of the ways we use punctuation when we speak.

Punctuation marks are simply signals, pointing out how the written language should be spoken.

Since there's no way to raise an eyebrow or put an inquiring tone of voice in writing, we let punctuation marks help do it for us.

PUNCTUATING SENTENCES

A sentence is a group of words that states a complete thought. To show its completeness, a sentence needs a definitely marked beginning and ending. *A sentence should begin with a capital letter and end with one of three strong marks of punctuation.*

- Periods speak matter of factly.
- Question marks leave you up in the air, don't they?
- Exclamation marks shout!

Use exclamation marks sparingly. Like any other attention-getting device, they tend to lose their power to attract if overused. Precise words and careful phrasing will do the job better than "noisy" punctuation.

Statements

Statements usually end with periods. For special emphasis, a writer may sometimes end a statement with an exclamation mark, but avoid overworking them.

1. In times of stress, people can become angry with their loved ones for no good reason.
2. Why, I am impressed by your store of information. (*Why* is used as an interjection in this sentence. It has no grammatical relation to the other words.)
3. I arrived at the box office early, but people already stood in line. (Note: This is a compound sentence. Can you pick out the subjects and verbs?)
4. Esteban asked when the post office closed. (This makes a statement about Esteban. It states the question he asked. It can also be called an indirect question.)

Commands

Commands may end in periods or exclamation marks, depending on how forcefully the writer wants to make his command.

1. Listen to me!
2. Please give me your attention.
3. Hurry up, and get ready. *OR* Hurry up, and get ready!
4. Bring your stereo, and I'll bring my new tapes. (Notice that one of the clauses in this compound sentence is a command.)

Questions

Questions always end with question marks.

1. Does the spaghetti sauce have enough oregano?
2. Why didn't you tell me earlier?
3. Where will you go, and what will you do?
4. Come here, or do I have to come after you?

Notice that both 3 and 4 are compound sentences. What is the S-V of the first clause in 4?

Exclamations

Exclamations always end in exclamation marks.

1. How generous you are!
2. Wow! What a great game that was!
3. What a wonderful time we had in Rome!
4. How dark it is, and how stormy!

Notice that "it is" is understood in the second part of sentence 4.

PUNCTUATING WITHIN SENTENCES

Separating Words and Word Groups
that Might Otherwise Be Confusing

1. Commas separate items in a series.

- Television, radio, and newspapers are the chief advertising media.
- The car roared down the street, around the corner, and through the alley at high speed. (Notice that *at high speed* is not part of the series of prepositional phrases.)
- You get out the chips and relish, I'll grill the burgers, and we'll soon be ready to eat.

Don't use a comma when only two words or phrases are joined by a coordinating conjunction, as *chips and relish* are. However, a comma is usually used between two clauses in a compound sentence.

2. Commas come after introductory phrases to create an attention-getting pause.

- Nevertheless, the experiment was a success.
- Well, you might have told me sooner.
- Still, there was no reason to be so angry about it.

but

- Still there was utter silence in the room.

3. Commas set off words added for identification.
   To identify a *place*:

- I was confused whether Josh meant London, England, or London, Ontario, Canada.

As in a series, the comma can be thought of as replacing an omitted word. With those words added: "I was confused whether Josh meant London in England or London in the province of Ontario in Canada."

Note: A pair of commas sets off words added for identification, such as *England*, when they come in the middle of a sentence.
To identify a *date*:

- July 4, 1776, is a date every American should remember.

With *nouns of address*:

- Mary, have you met Chet?
- This time, Al, you have gone too far!
- Do quit pacing for a minute, Lonnie.

A noun of address is simply the person spoken to directly. It has no real grammatical connection to a sentence.

To set off an *appositive*:

- Guy and his brother, Greg, look enough alike to be twins.
- Popinjay, my pet airedale, has very good manners.
- An expert on the psychology of successful executives, Dr. Clive Cleveland is today's speaker.
- The car, a Stutz Bearcat, is his most prized possession.

A noun in apposition renames and identifies the noun it's placed next to, but otherwise has no grammatical connection to a sentence. *Note*: Always be sure to use a pair of commas, both before and after, whenever the words marked off do not begin or end the sentence.

4. Commas set off the greeting and polite closing words of a letter.

- Dear Beth,
- Sincerely,

5. Commas set off parenthetical remarks.

- Of course, I agree with your point of view.
- Andrews, on the contrary, does not accept your theory.

6. One additional (and important) rule for commas: They may be used for clarity, according to the writer's own judgment.

Punctuation Is Also a Matter of Style

Newspapers and magazines have their own style sheets that state the rules they want their writers to follow. These rules for punctuation and capitalization vary in detail from publication to publication. A number of standard style books have been published and are available. Many dictionaries also have useful sections concerning punctuation.

Punctuating Compound Sentences

1. *A comma comes before the coordinating conjunction in a compound sentence of two clauses.*

   - The truckload of supplies arrived, but some of the packing crates were damaged.
   - You have your opinion, and I have mine.

2. *Punctuate compound sentences of two or more clauses like any other series.*

   - The mystery was solved, the lost keys were found, and we could finally be on our way.

3. *Alone, a semicolon is strong enough to join two independent clauses into a compound sentence.* With a "period" above and a "comma" below, a semicolon marks the halfway point in strength between a period and a comma.

   - In the past, a semicolon was used frequently; in the present, it has lost some of its popularity because of the shorter sentences now being favored.
   - Some writers of today freely join short independent clauses with commas; early grammar books call such sentences run-ons.

Four Possibilities for Two Independent Clauses

a. I already checked. I have no quarters.
b. I already checked, I have no quarters.
c. I already checked, and I have no quarters.
d. I already checked; I have no quarters.

It's the writer's choice!

KEEPING PUNCTUATION CLEAN

Punctuation should serve as a guide. It indicates pauses, tone, and emphasis. It provides signposts telling how to read a written message.

1. *Overused, punctuation takes away instead of adding effectiveness.*

   - The small boy, there, in the blue T-shirt, with Disney World on it, is sticking his finger, in the cake icing, and licking it off.
   - Do you mean it??? It can't be true!!! Really?!??

2. *Parentheses (like these) stop a reader while commas, as here, maintain the flow.* Parentheses are used to set off comments added to an already complete thought.

- They (that is, the words inside the curved lines) often seem an unnecessary afterthought.
- You must stop, read what's inside, then go back and read again (as if you'd been halted by a roadblock).

3. *You can use—but shouldn't overuse—dashes in a similar way.*

Ellipsis: When Something Is Missing but Understood

1. *Some things don't have to be said.* In the following sentences, notice that words have been omitted that the reader automatically understands and can supply. This is one type of ellipsis. (For a more detailed discussion, see p. 185.)

- Was the forecast for rain or sunshine tomorrow? Sunshine.
- No question about the answer. The forecast was for sunshine.
- There was no question about the answer, was there?

2. *Ellipsis is also punctuation.* Use three dots (. . .) to indicate a word or words have been left out.

- "When in the course of human events . . ." is the beginning of the Declaration of Independence.
- Grace said that she told you about . . . but you already know that, don't you?

Chapter 14

The 5 W's and an H

- Who
- What
- When
- Where
- Why
- How

These are questions every reporter learns from the very start. They form the basis of an interview. They are questions the reporter keeps in mind when writing the lead, or opening paragraph of a news story. After a while, they become second nature.

Just as in newswriting, the 5 W's and an H answer essential questions in grammar.

> *Who* or *what* is the sentence about?
>   . . . Finds the Subject
> Did or does *what*?
>   . . . Finds the Verb
> *Who* or *What*?
>   . . . Identifies all nouns and pronouns, including the subject
> *What* kind of?
>   . . . Is answered by an Adjective
> *Adverbs answer the other questions:*
>   When?
>   Where?
>   Why?
>   How?

ACTIVE READING

Reading is not just passing eyes over words and, like a camera, recording a mass of facts and information. The good reader is busy asking questions: Who or what? Is doing what? Where? When? How? Why? But the purpose is not simply to aid in picking out words and giving them grammatical labels; the questions also help find meaning.

And, when something is hard to understand, the good reader can turn to grammar. By identifying key words and seeing what questions they answer, someone who knows how grammar works can often arrive at an understanding of what even the most difficult-seeming sentences mean.

GRAMMAR IN ACTION

An understanding of grammar can help clarify the connection of ideas in all kinds of writing, from newspaper stories to poetry, from technical writing to fiction. To discover how grammar can help, read these lead paragraphs from a newspaper story.

CROWDED U.S. AIRPORTS THREATENED BY GRIDLOCK

The nation's major airports, a vast, varied, and aging collection of former farm fields and swamps, are rapidly approaching gridlock. The overworked facilities funnel more than 450 million passengers into high-flying jets traveling more than one-half billion miles annually.

According to experts, paralysis looms within five years and threatens the $57 billion-a-year airline industry, the nation's international competitiveness, countless local economies, and some fundamental assumptions about the American way of life.

Questioning the News Story

What is the S-V-C in Sentence #1?

(S-V-C) airports/are approaching/gridlock

What is the purpose of the words between "a vast" and "swamps"? *Collection* is the first noun you find in this phrase. An appositive, it's used to further identify airports.

What kind of collection?
Of fields and swamps

Grammar can help clear up the picture. The nation's airports are a vast, varied, and aging collection. They include former farm fields and swamps. They are fast approaching gridlock.

The S-V-C of Sentence #2 is

(S-V-C) Facilities/funnel/passengers

Where do they "funnel passengers"?

into jets

What kind of jets?

High-flying jets
Ones that travel more than one-half billion miles

When do they travel this distance?

annually

How and *why* are they overworked?

Sentence #3 of paragraph 2 says that "paralysis looms . . . and threatens." Threatens *what*? Four nouns answer the question: the *industry*, U.S. *competitiveness*, local *economies*, and some *assumptions*. The verb *threatens* has four complements. Going directly to them brings out these key points. To go further into the details, check the adjectives that modify each noun. Some sentences are packed with meaning. Grammar can help you strip them down to their essentials.

PRACTICE (WITH POETRY)

What are the "secrets" of a poem? Believe it or not, grammar often helps supply the answer, and it helps you get to the heart of poetry, too.

Part of the beauty of poetry is in seeing how the poet puts words together, using the order and balance of grammar to bring out the poem's meaning.

You don't have to know the definition of every word to understand what you read, nor should you take time to look up every word you don't know in the dictionary. Work from what you do know and, with the help of grammar, you can add to your vocabulary in the act of reading.

Read the following poem by Elinor Wylie. When you've finished the poem and the questions following it, you'll know why the poem itself isn't what you might expect from its title.

SEA LULLABY

The old moon is tarnished
With smoke of the flood,
The dead leaves are varnished
With color like blood,

A treacherous smiler   5
With teeth white as milk,
A savage beguiler
In sheathings of silk,

The sea creeps to pillage,
She leaps on her prey;   10
A child of the village
Was murdered today.

She came up to meet him
In a smooth golden cloak,
She choked him and beat him   15
To death, for a joke.

Her bright locks were tangled,
She shouted for joy,
With one hand she strangled
A strong little boy.   20

Now in silence she lingers
Beside him all night
To wash her long fingers
In silvery light.

1. What are the first two sets of subject/verb?

    a. (The) moon/is tarnished
    b. (The) leaves/are varnished

2. What words answer the question *how* for each?
3. The next subject/verb doesn't come until the third stanza:

    (S-V) (the) sea/creeps

What nouns in stanza two are used in apposition to *sea*?

4. Considering the title, what surprising adjectives describe these nouns and also the sea?

5. See how the S-Vs tell the story:

> She/leaps
> (A) child/was murdered
> She/came
> She/{choked (and) beat} him
> (Her) locks/were tangled
> She/shouted
> she/strangled/(a) boy

6. Working from the subjects, verbs, and complements, how does the poem answer the other 5 W's and an H about them?

7. The end of the poem states *she/lingers*.

> Where?
> When?
> Why?

8. What attitude does the poem create toward the boy? How?

9. The poem **personifies** the sea, speaking of it as if it were a woman and calling it *she*. What attitude does the poem create toward this "woman," the sea?

> What words describe its beauty?
> What words prove that the sea kills, not out of hate
>   but because it is in the sea's nature?

10. In what ways can the sea's behavior fit the idea of its "lullabying" the child, even though in a horrible way?

PUTTING YOUR KNOWLEDGE OF GRAMMAR TO WORK

Often the first, most important step in reading is to orient yourself by finding the S-V-C of problem sentences. This lets you know the underlying idea upon which the entire sentence is based.

The five W's and an H provide the answers that let you go on to ask further questions, such as

What is the author's purpose?
Why did he say that?
How does it all fit together?

Knowing the right questions is often just as important as knowing the answers. It gives you a place to start and somewhere to go.

At this point in grammar, there is still much to learn. In your reading, concentrate on determining meaningful answers to the 5 W's and an H. It's not necessary, or even helpful, to attempt to pinpoint the exact grammatical usage of every word or phrase.

Chapter 15

The Amazing Word *Be* and Its Many Faces

What do *is*, *was*, *am*, and *are* have in common? They are all forms of exactly the same verb, which goes by the family name *to be*. *Be* is the most irregular of all the irregular verbs. Its three principal parts are *be* (*am*, *is*, *are*), *was*, *been*. Other verbs, such as *go* (*go*, *went*, *gone*) and *eat* (*eat*, *ate*, *eaten*), also have parts that differ greatly from their root word or infinitive. Yet their family resemblance is much closer than those of *be*.

A DEFECTIVE VERB

How can such different-looking words actually be the same word? The dictionary calls *be* a defective verb because *be* gets its three principal parts from three unrelated stems.

Defective or not, *be* is in constant use and has many different purposes. It *does* work, and no one has ever gotten around to "fixing" it so that it works more smoothly.

Interestingly, the use of *be* in Black English comes closer to the pattern of most other verbs. It makes much more sense to say, "I be, you be, he be, we be," and so on than "I am, you are, he is, we are." Yet standard English accepts the irregularities of *be*, and it takes so much hard use (and sometimes abuse) that some people don't even realize it's all part of the same word.

Here are the proper forms of *be* in its primary and perfect tenses.

Present Tense

I am	We are
You are	You are
He/she/it is	They are

Past Tense

I was	We were
You were	You were
He/she/it was	They were

Future Tense

I will be	We will be
You will be	You will be
He/she/it will be	They will be

Present Perfect Tense

I have been	We have been
You have been	You have been
He/she/it has been	They have been

Past Perfect Tense

I had been	We had been
You had been	You had been
He/she/it had been	They had been

Future Perfect Tense

I will have been	We will have been
You will have been	You will have been
He/she/it will have been	They will have been

USES OF *BE*

Be is often used as a linking verb, but it's much more than that. The dictionary defines *be* as meaning to live, to happen, to remain or continue, or to belong to. In some sentences, it seems to mean to cost, to look, or to signify.

To understand how *be* works, consider its uses one by one.

Be Works as a Linking Verb

- Stephanie is an actress.
    (S-V-C) Stephanie/is/(an) actress
- Tom is handsome.
    (S-V-C) Tom/is/handsome
- Marty will be ready soon.
    (S-V-C) Marty/will be/ready
- Brad is my only brother.
    (S-V-C) Brad/is/brother

Actress and *brother* are nouns; *handsome* and *ready* are adjectives. All four words are subjective complements, which relate back to the subject. How do they differ from a complement like the following?

- The ball broke the window.
    (S-V-C) (The) ball/broke/window

Window takes the action of the subject/verb; it is therefore a direct object.

As a linking verb, *be* stresses the relationship between a subject and its complement. *Subjective complements* always follow the verb and come in the predicate, among words commonly related to each other in that part of the sentence. Subjective complements either describe or rename the subject.

In the previous examples, *actress* and *brother* are **predicate nouns**. *Handsome* and *ready* are **predicate adjectives**.

Other verbs work as linking verbs in the same way (for example, *seem* and *feel*), but none is put to work so often as *be*.

What Makes Up Complete Subjects and Predicates

- The colorful poster adds a touch of brightness to the room.
    (S-V-C) poster/adds/(a) touch

To know your way around in a sentence, it's best to find the subject and verb first. Then add on the complement, if there is one. Once you find these, it's easy to identify

1. **The complete subject**—the subject and all of its modifying words and phrases. Here: *The colorful poster*
2. **The complete predicate**—the word or words that tell what the subject of a sentence or clause did or was doing. It includes all modifying words and phrases. Here: *adds a touch of brightness to the room*

Here's how it works with a linking verb.

- The best feature of the car is its low mileage.
    (S-V-C) feature/is/mileage

In this sentence *is* is a linking verb and *mileage* is a predicate noun.

Complete subject	The best feature of the car
Complete predicate	is its low mileage

The subjective complement is always included in the predicate.

Be on the lookout for questions or other sentences in transposed order. Imagine them in natural order before trying to determine their complete subject and predicate.

- How does this new brand of toothpaste compare with your old one?
  (S-V) brand/does compare

The natural order is "This new brand of toothpaste does compare how with your old one."

Complete subject   This new brand of toothpaste
Complete predicate   does compare how with your old one

Be as an Intransitive Verb

- Your billfold is on the chest of drawers.
- Jake is in a hurry.
- Summer will be here soon.
- The performance is at 8 o'clock.

Notice that there is no answer if you say the verb and ask "what?" after it. Therefore, none of these sentences has a complement. All of the elements with the verb in the predicate work as adverbs. In all four sentences, *be* works as an intransitive verb (i.e., one that has no complement).

Note: Of course, *be* can take all the other helpers to form verb phrases: can be, will be, must be, would have been, should have been, might have been, and so on.

A Word About There

- Where is it? It is there.

Both of these sentences have the same S-V: it/is. Both *where* and *there* are adverbs.

Now consider these sentences.

- There is no question about it.
  (S-V) question/is
- There is a prediction of snow for tomorrow.
  (S-V) prediction/is

In neither sentence does *there* answer the question "Where?" What work is it doing, then?

In both sentences, *there* works as an introductory word, to fill out the sentence and act as a balance on one side of the verb *be* for the subject on the other. In such sentences, it's not an adverb. It's called an *expletive*; its job is to let the subject come later. Don't be fooled into calling it the subject.

PRACTICE

Identify the S-V-C or S-V of each sentence to find whether *be* is used as a linking or intransitive verb. If *be* has a complement, decide whether it's a predicate noun or a predicate adjective.

1. Ernie is the team's leading scorer.
2. Paula has always been very good at tennis.
3. Someday Matt will be either in an executive suite or in prison.
4. Lan, you can be so difficult at times.
5. There might not be enough food for everyone at the party.
6. Julie would have been my choice for the job.
7. Be careful of that slippery spot on the sidewalk.

(For answers, see page 197.)

PROGRESSIVE VERB PHRASES

What is the difference in meaning between each of the following pairs?

Andy talks	Andy is talking
Bea swims	Bea is swimming
Cathy laughs	Cathy is laughing
you practice	you are practicing
I drive	I am driving
they go	they are going

Although both deal with the present, the second set tells of an action "in progress." The first, actually in the present tense, tells of a habitual act.

Be + the *-ing* form of the verb = the **progressive**

The *-ing* form of the verb is called the **present participle**.

Be works as a helper to determine the time of the action "in progress" that the present participle shows.

progressive present

I am working; he/she/it is working; we/you/they are working

progressive past

I, he/she/it was working; we/you/they were working

progressive future

I/they will be working

progressive present perfect

I/we/you/they have been working; he/she/it has been working

progressive past perfect

I/they had been working

progressive future perfect

I/they will have been working

Forming the Present Participle

There's no trick to forming the present participle. Just add *-ing* to the base of the verb. Even *be* is regular; it becomes *being*.

Some verbs, such as *get*, *sit*, and *bat* double their final consonant to keep the short sound of a vowel: *getting*, *sitting*, and *batting*. Others drop an *e* before *-ing*. Examples are *become*, *rate*, and *bite*. Their present participles are *becoming*, *rating*, and *biting*. Just compare *matting* with *mating* to see why such changes are necessary.

When in doubt, check the dictionary. As with other verb forms, if the *-ing* form isn't listed, you may assume it's regular.

When a verb is progressive, there are always two or more words in its verb string. A present participle that tells what the subject does or is doing comes last. As with any verbs, the progressive may or may not have a complement. It can be transitive, intransitive, or linking.

Examples

- Chet has been working at the Blanchard Company for three years.
  (S-V) Chet/has been working
  Intransitive—has no object

- Joyce is buying a new car, a Jeep Wagoneer.
  (S-V-C) Joyce/is buying/(a) car
  Transitive—has a direct object, *car*
- The defense witness was being very hesitant about all of his answers.
  (S-V-C) (The) witness/was being/hesitant
  Linking—has a complement, *hesitant* (a predicate adjective)

PRACTICE

Identify the S-V-C or S-V of each sentence. Determine which verbs are intransitive, transitive, and linking. If there is a complement, decide whether it is a direct object, predicate adjective, or predicate noun.

1. We are counting on you for help.
2. Nora and Ted have been saving their money for a new house.
3. For a change, the baby was being an absolute angel.
4. The company will be using a new phone system in the future.
5. You are really promising a great deal.
6. Without our knowledge, a chipmunk had been nibbling blossoms off the plants.
7. In a few minutes, we will have been waiting for Jed for exactly two hours.
8. For a change, the restless children were being quiet.

(For answers, see page 197.)

THE PASSIVE VOICE

Verbs do more than express meaning. You've seen how they express time or tense. They also have a quality called *voice*. Verbs have two voices, *active* and *passive*.

Voice is easiest to understand when you see it in action.

a. The committee chose Kyle as Salesperson of the Year.
   (S-V-C) committee/chose/Kyle
b. Kyle was chosen as Salesperson of the Year by the committee.
   (S-V) Kyle/was chosen

Example (a) is active; the subject/verb is acting upon the object, *Kyle*. Example (b) is passive. The former object is now a subject and passively "takes" the action of the verb. The subject in (a) is now the object of a preposition. In example (b), the verb still answers the question, "Did what?" about the subject, *Kyle*.

Of course, only a verb that can take an object (i.e., a transitive verb) works in the passive voice.

Why Does English Need a Passive Voice?

Some might answer that it doesn't. Some writers try hard to avoid using the passive voice, because they want their work to sound active.

Notice the disadvantages of the passive voice.

a. The writer gave a wrong percentage in the article.
b. A wrong percentage was given in the article by the writer.
c. A wrong percentage was given in the article.

It takes (b) eleven words to say exactly the same thing that (a) says in nine. Sentence (c) uses only eight words, but omits information that may be important.

In addition, passive voice doesn't carry the idea forward as forcefully as the active voice does.

There are, however, advantages to the passive voice. The first question to ask about a sentence is, "Who or what is it about?" In example (b), the answer is *percentage*. In example (a), active voice makes it *writer*.

Word order is important in English, and the passive voice gives an "up front" position to a word that would come after the verb in the active voice. *Passive voice turns the receiver of an action into the subject.* It turns an object into a subject.

In this case, *writer* isn't very important (all articles have writers), so (c) is probably the best sentence of the three. But if you want to emphasize a particular writer as being at fault, active voice is preferable.

- (weak) The wrong percentage was given by Friedman in his article.
- (better) Friedman gave the wrong percentage in his article.

The passive voice works best when the agent or former subject is nonessential to the sentence. In any case, avoid its overuse.

passive voice = the helping verb *be* + the past participle of the verb

1. Use *be* in the same tense in which the basic verb would be in the active voice.
2. The past participle is the third principal part of the verb.

Examples

Note the changes in subject/verb in the following.

1. (*Active*) Senator Bacon gave the keynote address at the convention.
   (*Passive*) The keynote address at the convention was given by Senator Bacon.
2. (*Active*) We have not revealed our plans to anyone.
   (*Passive*) Our plans have not been revealed to anyone.
3. (*Active*) Heavy air traffic causes long delays at the nation's major airports.
   (*Passive*) Long delays at the nation's airports are caused by heavy air traffic.

PRACTICE

Identify the S-V-C or S-V of each sentence, and decide whether the voice is active or passive. Put each sentence in the voice opposite to its version below. Notice that the agent of the action is often missing from the passive voice. In this case, supply a subject in the active voice.

1. The lawyer questioned Sylvia about her whereabouts on the night of May 17.
2. Many of the regular shows were not televised Monday because of the play-offs.
3. People around the world will have heard the news at almost the same instant.
4. The latest pictures of Harry's grandson are shown to everyone.
5. The Oscar for best picture will be given last.
6. Most of the chocolate cake was eaten by my little brother.
7. I have spoken my last word on the subject.

(For answers, see page 197.)

Chapter 16

More about Nouns and Pronouns

Personal pronouns spell trouble for many people. They're a marvelous invention to take the place of nouns, but the fact that each has several forms can cause confusion.

People choose and use the wrong pronouns for a number of reasons.

- They may not understand how pronouns work.
- They may have a habit of using pronouns incorrectly and find it hard to break, although they do "know better."
- They may even think the correct forms sound too stuffy and artificial to modern ears. Yet even in conversation, certain mistakes in pronouns act just like a spot of ketchup on a new outfit: They spoil the effect completely.

CASES

Case #1

A noun or pronoun used as **subject** of a sentence or clause

Who or what it's all about

or as **predicate noun**

follows a linking verb and renames the subject

is in the **nominative case**.

Case #2

A noun or pronoun used as **direct object**

receives the action of the predicate verb

or as **object of a preposition** is in the **objective case**. (Other objective case uses will fall naturally into place if you understand these.)

Here is a table of pronouns that change according to case (*you* and *it* don't change).

Singular	Nominative Case	Objective Case
1st Person	I	me
2nd Person	you	you
3rd Person	he, she, it	him, her, it
Plural		
1st Person	we	us
2nd Person	you	you
3rd Person	they	them

Making the Right Choice

In English, nouns don't have different forms for the nominative and objective case, but personal pronouns do. That's why it's so important to know *how* a pronoun works to be sure *which* to choose.

Explain the following choices of pronouns, according to how the nouns work in the first sentence of each pair.

a. Helen hates Herbert.
   She hates him.
b. We bought a wedding present for Carol and Ken.
   We bought a wedding present for her and him.
c. My friends and I disagree about the use of nuclear power.
   They and I disagree about it.
d. The caller was Sidney.
   The caller was he.

That last sentence (like *It was I*) may sound strange and artificial, but using the nominative case of the pronoun in place of a predicative noun *is* the right choice, according to the way the pronoun is working. Should you sound stuffy and be right, or informal and "wrong"? Modern speakers who know their grammar sometimes rephrase a sentence, just to avoid such a decision.

Today's informal usage okays the objective case after a linking verb. It approves no other exception. Choosing and using pronouns correctly is an important mark of being good in grammar.

More about the Objective Case

So far, you have seen two kinds of objects: direct object and object of a preposition. There are three more ways verbs make objects of nouns and pronouns.

Indirect Object

- Nan brought her hosts a bottle of wine.
    Brought <u>whom</u> or <u>what</u>?
    Both <u>hosts</u> and <u>bottle</u>

The second is a direct object, the first an **indirect object**, which names *to* or *for* whom an action is being done. (Notice that the sentence "works" without its indirect object, but doesn't without the second.) How can you be sure you've found an indirect object?

a. Indirect objects come before a direct object.
b. You can turn the indirect object into an object of a preposition, using *to* or *for*.

- Nan brought a bottle of wine for her hosts.

c. Only certain verbs can take indirect objects. They include *give, take, bring, offer,* and *tell.*

- Clark told the police officer the truth.
- The boss has offered Andrea a promotion.
- Give me your attention.

Objective Complement

- The Liars Club elected Trixie president.
    Elected *whom* or *what*? Trixie
    Elected her *what*? President

In this sentence, the direct object comes first, and its complement follows.

a. The **objective complement** renames the object, just as a subjective complement renames or modifies the subject.
b. Objective complements can also be adjectives.

- Are you calling me lazy?

c. Only certain verbs can have objective complements. They include *name*, *choose*, *consider*, and *label*.

- Jazz fans consider Art Tatum a piano genius.
- The team has chosen Brenda captain.
- Some people would label Theo a loner.

d. Check by putting *as* or *to be* between the direct object and its noun objective complement. It ought to make sense.

Retained Object

- Andrea has been offered a promotion.
- Art Tatum is considered a piano genius.
- Theo would be labeled a loner by some people.

These sentences come from the examples for indirect objects and objective complements. In each, the verb is now in the passive voice, and one of the objects has become a subject. Here are the (S-V)'s of those sentences.

- Andrea/has been offered
- Art Tatum/is considered
- Theo/would be labeled

Since verbs in passive voice can no longer have objects, the "left-overs" (*promotion*, *genius*, and *loner*) are called **retained objects**. It means their sense as objects is kept, even though the verb isn't active.

It's another example of the importance of word order to English. If a sentence in the passive voice is difficult to understand, it's often helpful to change its word order and consider it in active voice, thereby clarifying its meaning. Only sentences that would have indirect objects or objective complements in the active voice can have retained objects.

Word Order Makes English Work

What words are nouns? verbs? adjectives? Without a sentence, it's nearly impossible to say for sure. Is *light*, for instance, a noun? It all depends.

- The light was dazzling.
     light as a noun

- Fireworks light up the sky.
    . . . as a verb
- Bring a light jacket.
    . . . as an adjective
- The child skipped lightly.
    . . . and with a slight change, an adverb!

In some languages, it's much easier to identify a part of speech by word endings or inflections, but in English you need to see a word at work before you can tell.

To discover the possible uses of a word, check in the dictionary.

PRACTICE

The use of nouns and pronouns is hardest to figure out when they're compound. The following sentences should be a challenge. First, identify the S-V-C at the heart of each sentence. Then list every noun and pronoun, along with its use in the sentence. Watch for compound usage.

1. Between you and me, we will make the project a success.
2. Both Bob and I have brought enough potato salad for a thousand hungry ants.
3. According to Mr. Walsh, a guarantee on the brake job was given his wife and him by the mechanic.
4. In sports and world affairs, people are too often divided into us and them.
5. Gloria, are you and he kidding, or are you really calling me a procrastinator?

(For answers, see page 197.)

MORE PRACTICE

Determine the case use of the word that should fill the blank space before making a choice.

1. With Rob and _____ (she, her) as candidates, it will be a difficult choice.
2. What can I bring you and _____ (they, them) from Paris?
3. Along with Sue and _____ (she, her), Nat gave Trish and _____ (I, me) a sample of his homemade microwave brownies.

4. Without a doubt, both _____ (he, him) and _____ (I, me) were interested in Larry's suggestion.

5. Neither Paula nor _____ (he, him) would be my choice for the position.

(For answers, see page 198.)

POSSESSIVES

How do the underlined words work in the following sentences? What questions do they answer?

- That is <u>Mario's</u> jacket.
- The <u>boys'</u> bedroom is a mess.
- What is <u>your</u> opinion?

All three seem to answer the question *"What one?"* Therefore, they do the work of an adjective.

Some grammarians, basing their description of English on the grammar of ancient Latin and Greek, would say that these examples belong to a third case of nouns, the possessive case. Actually, many words well known as nouns in English often show up as adjectives, even without a change of ending.

- The <u>storm</u> clouds hung overhead and darkened the sky.
- Our brains are our <u>message</u> center.

It's easier, in fact, to see possessives as nouns acting as adjectives. Their purpose is to indicate ownership or belonging.

Possessive Forms

In the possessive singular, noun forms take an apostrophe followed by an *s*: *author's* imagination, *boy's* dream, *horse's* speed, *Dad's* luck, *engineer's* opinion, and so on.

In the plural, most just add an apostrophe after their regular sign of the plural, *s*: *farmers'* crops, *Giants'* victory, *cats'* personalities, *Indians'* raid, *jokers'* pranks, and so on. To plurals that don't end in *s*, an *s* is added after an apostrophe: *children's* mittens, *women's* viewpoints, *sheep's* wool, *geese's* formation, *deer's* coloring, and so on. *When in doubt, check the dictionary*; it will help with irregular forms for plurals.

Personal pronouns have two forms to use as possessives. The first is for use as an *adjective*:

	Singular	*Plural*
1st Person	my	our
2nd Person	your	your
3rd Person	his, her, its	their

The second is for use *in place of a noun*:

	Singular	*Plural*
1st Person	mine	ours
2nd Person	yours	yours
3rd Person	his, hers, its	theirs

Note that both *his* and *its* stay the same, whether used as possessive adjectives or pronouns.

Here are some possessives in action. Where are your crayons? Those are mine; this box is his. Hers has more colors than yours or mine. Let's share ours. Buddy and Bonnie forgot theirs. Which are pronouns and which are adjectives?

Possessive noun forms also work two ways: Sarah's hair is blond; Lou's is a bit darker.

A Warning about Apostrophes

None of the possessive pronoun forms should be used with an apostrophe. Check the use of the following:

The dog's leash is hanging behind the door.
Its leash is hanging behind the door.
Is this Vicki's billfold?
Is this her billfold?
Is this hers?

With personal pronouns, apostrophes replace missing letters in contractions. For example:

I'm = I am	you're = you are	it's = it is
I've = I have	he'd = he had	we'll = we will

Be sure you can substitute *it is* or *it has* before you write *it's*.

- I like that song, but I can never remember its name.

In this case, *its* is correct. You don't mean *it is name*.

- It's by the Beatles.

It is by the Beatles. The apostrophe is correctly used. Other frequently confused pairs are *your* and *you're*, and *their* and *they're*.

   Remember that it's important to use an apostrophe in contractions (*it's* the right way to make short work of *it is*). But a personal pronoun never uses an apostrophe to form its possessive (*its* formation of the possessive is different from a noun's).

Chapter 17

Introducing the Verbals: The Participles Are Coming!

grow (grö), v.i. [GREW (gröö), GROWN (grön), GROWING]—Also, v.t.

This is how the dictionary lists the principal parts of the irregular verb *grow*, along with their pronunciation. The principal parts of regular verbs such as *talk* (talked, talked, talking) aren't in the dictionary.

THE PARTICIPLES HAVE COME!

It's easier to see how the principal parts work with an irregular verb such as *grow*. The third principal part of the verb is called the **past participle**. It *always* needs a helper to act as a verb. It's used in the perfect tenses and in passive voice.

- Danny <u>has</u> grown.
- Soybeans <u>are</u> grown by many Midwest farmers.

The *-ing* form, or present participle, works with *be* in all the progressive verb phrases (see Chapter 15).

- We are growing.
- We will be growing.
- We had been growing.

Both of these verb forms are called participles. You can think of the term *participle* as showing that they are just *part* of a verb phrase and need a helper to be included in the S-V-C. Or you can remember that the word *participle* derives from "participate" and that a participle "takes part" in a sentence.

With a regular verb, it isn't possible to identify a past participle unless it's at work in a sentence.

- We walked and walked.
- We had walked for miles.
- The dog was walked by his master.

PARTICIPLES AS ADJECTIVES

Now, for the "magic" of word order.

- The baby is <u>crying</u>.
    (S-V) (The) baby/is crying
- The baby wants attention.
    (S-V-C) (The) baby/wants/attention
- The <u>crying</u> baby wants attention.

Presto! The participle is now taking part in the sentence as an adjective.

Notice how it still carries the idea of action. Participles used as adjectives can be easily seen as carrying the idea of a simple sentence.

- The masterpiece had been stolen.
- The police returned the masterpiece to its owner.
- The police returned the <u>stolen</u> masterpiece to its owner.

PARTICIPIAL PHRASES

- We were coming back from California.
- We stopped for a few days in Las Vegas.
- <u>Coming back from California</u>, we stopped for a few days in Vegas.

- I am wearing a ring.
- The ring was given to me by my great aunt.
- I am wearing a ring <u>given to me by my great aunt</u>.

"Coming back from California" and "Given to me by my great aunt" are called **participial phrases**.

The words in phrases always work together as one part of speech, and the participial phrases in these sentences work as adjectives.

It helps to think of a participial phrase as a former sentence with its subject and helping verbs chopped off so it can be combined with another clause.

- I am wearing a ring given to me by my great aunt.
  (S-V-C) I/am wearing/(a) ring

What ring? (One that was) given to me by my great aunt. The entire phrase works as an *adjective*. Both *to me* and *by my great aunt* are prepositional phrases modifying *given*.

Because it also has qualities of a verb, a participle can do what ordinary adjectives can't.

- Bernie was showing her sense of humor.
  (S-V-C) Bernie/was showing/sense
- Bernie did not take the remark seriously.
  (S-V-C) Bernie/did take/(the) remark

    Go together as

- <u>Showing her sense of humor</u>, Bernie did not take the remark seriously.

Yes, *sense* is still an object in the last sentence.

When can an adjective take an object? When it's a word that can also work as a verb, such as a participle. Even when it works as an adjective, a present or past participle can still have objects and modifiers, just as it does when it's part of a verb phrase.

PRACTICE

Identify the participles and participial phrases working as adjectives, as well as the nouns or pronouns they modify.

1. Typed in red, the manuscript hurt my eyes.
2. His smiling face hid his wounded pride.
3. The clouds, driven by the wind, were a sign of the changing weather.
4. A coded message held the secret of the missing treasure.
5. Anyone knowing the truth should doubt the company's boasting claims for its product.

6. Wearing that color, you look exceptionally attractive.
7. No one ever recovered the money stolen in the robbery.

(For answers, see page 198.)

PARTICIPLES IN ACTION

Poet and critic John Ciardi said good poetry contains more verbs than adjectives. Participles have the qualities of both. In the following poem by Frank Marshall Davis, notice the use of present participles to create an active picture of the night. Be sure to identify the subject, verb, and complement of each sentence to make the picture clear.

FOUR GLIMPSES OF NIGHT

1

Eagerly
Like a woman hurrying to her lover
Night comes to the world
And lies, yielding and content
Against the cool round face
Of the moon.

2

Night is a curious child, wandering
Between earth and sky, creeping
In windows and doors, daubing
The entire neighborhood
With purple paint.
Day
Is an apologetic mother
Cloth in hand
Following after.

3

Peddling
From door to door
Night sells
Black bags of peppermint stars
Heaping cones of vanilla moon
Until
His wares are gone
Then shuffles homeward
Jingling the gray coins
Of daybreak.

4

Night's brittle song, silver-thin
Shatters into a billion fragments
Of quiet shadows
At the blaring jazz
Of the morning sun.

Avoid Dangling and Misplaced Participles

- Flying to California, we saw the Grand Canyon.
- We saw the Grand Canyon, flying to California.
- Flying to California, the Grand Canyon was seen.

The last two sentences imply that the Grand Canyon was flying. Because of the importance of word order, a reader assumes that a participle is meant to describe whatever is closest. When a word is missing or a participle is carelessly placed, confusion results.

Don't be guilty of dangling or misplacing a participle. It sounds silly, and many consider it a serious crime against good grammar.

Note: Don't ask a participial phrase to modify a possessive.

- (wrong) Jumping up, Ozzie's reaction was instant.
    A *reaction* can't jump.
- (right) Jumping up, Ozzie reacted instantly.

THE GERUND: ANOTHER VERSATILE VERBAL

- Sailing, swimming, and water-skiing are popular water sports.

Without a second thought, most people would say that *sailing*, *swimming*, and *water-skiing* are nouns. Of course, they'd be right. Together, those words make up the compound subject of the sentence.

But, notice the *-ing* endings. Although they're often taken for granted, such nouns are also verb forms. All can serve as adjectives, too, as in "*sailing* ship," "*swimming* expert," and "*water-skiing* enthusiast." But only the *-ing* form of the participle can work as a noun; when it does, it's called a *gerund*.

What's the difference between a gerund and present participle? None at all, in the way they look; you can only tell when one's at work.

The following sentences contain present participles at work in verb strings.

a. You will be joining us.
   (S-V-C) You/will be joining/us
b. We have been doing the job carefully.
   (S-V-C) We/have been doing/(the) job
c. I am keeping a journal.
   (S-V-C) I/am keeping/(a) journal

Compare them with the following, which look the same, but are now gerunds.

d. Thank you for joining us.
e. Doing the job carefully can often save time in the long run.
f. You should try keeping a journal.

Gerunds will always answer the noun question, *what*? (since they name an action, they don't answer to *who*?).

Doublecheck a gerund by testing another noun or pronoun in its place. In d, *joining us* is an object of a preposition; in e, *Doing the job carefully* is the subject, and in f, *keeping a journal* is the direct object.

Being verbals, gerunds not only work as nouns. They can also have objects and be modified by adverbs and adverb phrases. In the examples, *carefully* is an adverb modifying *Doing*, and all three gerunds have direct objects.

The -ing form of the verb, which expresses an action "in progress," is the only one that works as a noun, or gerund.

PRACTICE

As sentences become more complicated, it's more important than ever to remember the first step in grammar: Find the subject-verb-complement.

In the following sentences, you'll find the past or present participle working as (1) part of a verb phrase, (2) an adjective, or (3) a gerund. Some sentences contain more than one verbal.

- Being sure of the S-V-C will make the job easier!
  (S-V-C) Being sure/will make/(the) job

1. We are having trouble with our old car.
2. Keeping it in working order is almost a full-time job.
3. We have been thinking of selling the rattling old collection of scrap metal.
4. You could almost pity the poor old thing, broken down by many miles of driving.
5. In a joking way, we sometimes talk of retiring it.
6. Judging by its resale value, the worthless thing deserves being junked.
7. Loved by no one, wanted by no one, our old car is facing a future as dim as its failing headlights.

   (For answers, see page 198.)

A Fine Point of Grammar

Because a gerund is a noun, it may also need a possessive adjective.

Example A
- Being tired can cause carelessness.
- Bill's being tired caused his carelessness.

Bill's modifies the gerund subject, *being tired*. You should also say

- His being tired caused his carelessness.

   The gerund could, of course, be turned into a participial phrase:

- Bill, being tired, was careless.

Example B
   The following set works in the same way as Example A.

- Talking with the manager brought immediate results.
- Our talking with the manager brought immediate results.
- The customer, talking with the manager, explained the problem.

TO BE OR NOT TO BE: THE INFINITIVE

The infinitive is known as the simple form of the verb—simply because it doesn't express the notion of tense or time. In English, *to* is the sign of the infinitive, but it's not the preposition *to*.

To the store is a prepositional phrase that works as an adjective or adverb. *To go* is an infinitive. Like the other verbals, it can work as a(n)

Noun: To go seemed difficult.
Adjective: That's the place to go.
Adverb: We were waiting to go.

As other verbal phrases, an infinitive phrase can include objects and adverbial modifiers:

- We hope to go early in the morning.

The infinitive can also have a subject, *but* the subject of the infinitive is in the objective case:

- The boss expects me to prepare a report on our sales prospects.

To get a better understanding of how infinitives work, compare the following pairs of sentences. See how infinitives work as various parts of speech.

Infinitives as Nouns

Example 1
- They want a <u>house</u> in the country.
    (S-V-C) They/want/(a) house
- They want <u>to buy a place in the country</u>.
    The entire infinitive phrase is the object of
        want, as the noun *house* was in the first
        example. *Place* is the direct object of *to buy*.

Example 2
- Do you expect <u>a miracle</u>?
    (S-V-C) you/do expect/(a) miracle
- Do you expect <u>me to know the answer</u>?
    me to know the answer = object of *expect*
    me = subject of the infinitive
    answer = its object

Infinitives as Adjectives

Example 1

- The horse <u>in the lead</u> is Swift Eagle.
  (S-V-C) horse/is/Swift Eagle
  in the lead = prepositional phrase, adjective
- The horse <u>to watch</u> is Swift Eagle.
  to watch = infinitive, adjective

Example 2

- This is the car stereo <u>for you</u>.
  (S-V-C) This/is/(the) stereo
- This is the only car stereo <u>to feature such high quality at a low price</u>.

Infinitives as Adverbs

Example 1

- We stayed up <u>late</u>.
  (S-V) We/stayed
- We stayed up <u>to watch the late news</u>.

Example 2

- The guard patrolled the gate <u>constantly</u>.
- The guard patrolled the gate <u>to prevent outsiders from entering</u>.

The Expletive It: *The Secret Is Knowing the Right Question*

- It is my ambition to be a lawyer.

  1. What is *it*?
  2. What is the subject of the sentence?
  3. *Who* or *what* is the sentence about? That's easy. *My ambition*—which
     is therefore the subject.

- My ambition is to be a lawyer.
  Then *to be a lawyer* is a predicate noun.

It isn't always a pronoun. Sometimes it's simply an introductory word, called an expletive. In this case, it doesn't really take the place of a noun or have a complement.

- It takes time to do good work. (To do good work takes time.)

The subject is *to do good work*; *it* is an expletive. Remember, *there* has a similar use in sentences. For example: There is reason to be thankful.

PRACTICE

a. Identify the S-V-C's.
b. Pick out the infinitive phrases, and decide if they are used as nouns, adjectives, or adverbs.
c. If the infinitive works as a noun, determine its specific use in the sentence.
d. Note whether the infinitive phrase itself has a subject, object, or other modifiers.

1. The team tried to make the short yardage by rushing.
2. Lou was hurrying to be there on time.
3. I need a gift to please someone difficult to please.
4. To like oneself is important.
5. Children need someone to be their role models.
6. We have been waiting to hear the judges' decision.
7. His dream has always been to travel in space.

(For answers, see page 198.)

A Few Infinitives Work Without To

- The wind made the curtains flutter.
- Did you hear him sing?
- We will let them help.

Change the verb *made* to *caused*, *did hear* to *did ask*, and *let* to *allow*. See how the sign of the infinitive *to* appears naturally.

And Infinitives, like other verbals, can dangle!

- To speak frankly, that color is not flattering to you. (Can colors speak?)
- To speak frankly, I think that color is really *you*.

Grammar is a way of discovering how language works best. It's not a way of forcing language to do anything. English is ever expanding and changing. It's becoming simpler in some ways and more complicated in others.

It's not necessary to worry about the "picky" details of grammar. Gerunds, participles, and infinitives have baffled many. Consider yourself lucky if they make sense to you.

Don't make yourself work at grammar, make grammar work for you. Make your first goal be to find the subject/verb. If you do, you'll always know what's really happening in any sentence.

Chapter 18

More Punctuation: I Said, "May I Have Your Attention, Please?"

Punctuation is an attention-getting device. Yet its purpose is not to call attention to itself but to clarify other points in a sentence, such as its ending.

Capitalization works in much the same way. It's not really intended to be a chore or a challenge. Both punctuation and capital letters should help carry a message along more smoothly, not cause road bumps or confusion. When punctuation is correct, you probably aren't even aware of it.

Punctuation marks call attention to themselves only when they ar'ent in the right place: or when there missing overused—or sending a faulty signal???!!!???

Oops! . . . when they aren't in the right place or when they're missing, overused, or sending a faulty signal.

Punctuation Helps Make Sentences Clear

what would it be like without punctuation marks it would be terrible the reader would have to stop and try to puzzle out when a sentence or complete thought ended no one would know for sure whether the cowboys were a group of range riders or a football team they might think sixty minutes was a period of time instead of a television program

the problems go on *but there's no way to stop without a period.*

HOW QUOTATION MARKS WORK

Quotation marks are used to call attention to something "different" in a sentence. Their most frequent use is to surround the exact words that someone is saying or has written.

Understanding how quotation marks work can help make you a better reader. There's little call for them in everyday writing, but it's important to know who's speaking when you read.

The two elements of a quotation are

1. Something said
   "It's too bad that you must leave so soon."
   "Are you sure you must go?"
2. Someone saying it
   Davina said *or* said Davina

Plus, of course, a bit more punctuation. Quotations allow plenty of room for variety. *Identification* of the speaker can come *first*:

- Davina said, "It's too bad that you must leave so soon." *Note*: Identification is set off by a comma.
- Davina asked, "Are you sure you must go?" *Note*: End punctuation for the words spoken comes within the quotation marks.

Identification can come at the *end*.

- "It's too bad that you must leave so soon," Davina said.
- "Are you sure you must go?" asked Davina.

Note: A single quoted statement needs only a comma, then quotation marks, before the identification. The only period goes at the very end. A quoted question requires its own question mark inside quotation marks and no comma after.

Identification can come in the *middle* of a quotation.

- "It's too bad," said Davina, "that you must leave so soon."
- "Are you sure," she asked, "that you must go?"

Note: In the middle of a sentence, the identification is set off by commas. Notice their placement in relation to the quotation marks that signal when the quote stops and then begins again. Since the second half of the quote does not begin a sentence, it does not begin with a capital letter.

Two or more quoted sentences can be included inside a single pair of quotation marks.

- "It's too bad that you must leave so soon. Are you sure you must go?" Davina asked.
- "It's too bad that you must leave so soon," said Davina. "Are you sure you must go?"

Notice how the first sentence ends with a period, after *Davina*, and the following sentence stands by itself in the paragraph.

Of course, the identification can have its own modifiers:

■ The girl in the trenchcoat shrugged and said doubtfully, "Well, if you say so."

Unless other words are necessary, well-known writers stick to just plain *said*—not *whispered*, *shouted*, or *gasped*. After all, the important part of a quotation *is* the quotation.

READING DIALOGUE

As you read, keep the following in mind.

1. A new paragraph begins every time there is a change in speaker.
2. It's rare for one speech to continue for more than one paragraph. If it does, the quotation mark will be missing at the end of all but the last paragraph, although one will begin the next. A quotation mark at the end of the paragraph means the end of the speech. Charles Dickens in *A Tale of Two Cities* makes an entire chapter of a letter, quoting a man's story of his false imprisonment. The chapter opens with a quotation mark—each paragraph starts with one, too—but only with the end of the chapter does the closing quotation mark come.
3. The good reader concentrates on the conversation and only checks on the identification to make sure he knows who's speaking.
4. Identification is often left out completely when it's clear who's speaking. When just two people are speaking, each new paragraph signals a switch in speaker.

QUOTATION MARKS IN ACTION

Here is a sample of John Steinbeck's masterful use of dialogue. Steinbeck reveals what his characters are like by letting them speak for themselves. In this selection from *Of Mice and Men*, George is trying to keep Lennie from saying anything to spoil their chances of getting a job as ranch hands.

Notice Steinbeck's use of quotation marks, identification, and paragraphing to make the course of conversation clear.

> *. . . The boss licked his pencil. "What's your name?"*
> *"George Milton."*
> *"And what's yours?"*
> *George said, "His name's Lennie Small."*

The names were entered in the book. "Le's see, this is the twentieth, noon the twentieth." He closed the book. "Where you boys been working?"

"Up around Weed," said George.

"You, too?" to Lennie.

"Yeah, him too," said George.

The boss pointed a playful finger at Lennie. "He ain't much of a talker, is he?"

"No, he ain't, but he's sure a hell of a good worker. Strong as a bull."

Lennie smiled to himself. "Strong as a bull," he repeated.

George scowled at him, and Lennie dropped his head in shame at having forgotten.

The boss said suddenly, "Listen, Small!" Lennie raised his head. "What can you do?"

In a panic, Lennie looked at George for help. "He can do anything you tell him," said George. "He's a good skinner. He can rassel grain bags, drive a cultivator. He can do anything. Just give him a try."

The boss turned on George. "Then why don't you let him answer?. . . "

PRACTICE

Supply quotation marks and other necessary punctuation.

1. Wade said I hope you understand my point of view
2. Please give me one more chance Bert begged
3. Dan declared I need more time to think
4. What are you doing asked Alice
5. I am on my hands and knees explained Ed to look for my lost contact lens
6. His actions confused me too replied Ruth
7. Just listen to my side of the story Paul pleaded
8. Ted told Terry you have the wrong idea
9. Look out cried Cathy you're going to run into that door
10. Someone watching observed Otis wouldn't understand this at all

(For answers, see page 198.)

MORE WAYS TO USE QUOTATION MARKS

1. *To enclose titles of short pieces:* short stories, poems, articles, chapters, and so on.

   ▪ Have you read Elinor Wylie's poem, "Sea Lullaby"?

2. *To set off words used in a special way* in order to call attention to them or explain them.

- Many computer terms, such as "input" and "feedback," are now used in everyday conversation.

ITALIC LETTERS

In handwriting, typing, and some computer print-outs underlining stands for a word or words that would be set in italics, if professionally printed.

1. *Italics set off the titles of books* and other long written works.

- *The Grapes of Wrath* by John Steinbeck makes the suffering of migrant farmers come to life.

2. *Italics emphasize words to be stressed*, such as possibly unfamiliar foreign words and phrases.

- Judd considers himself a *bon vivant.*

3. *Italics highlight words used as words* instead of carrying their usual meaning.

- When spoken, sound-alikes such as *there, their*, and *they're* are impossible to tell apart without a sentence.

4. *Italics set apart special names* given to ships, planes, and racing cars.

- His boat, *The Breakaway*, is docked at the sailing club.

THE COLON

Use a colon after a statement introducing a list, explanation, or illustration.

- In grammar, always remember to do the following first: find the subject/ verb.

Note: Do not use a colon to introduce words that complete a statement and are actually part of the subject/verb/complement themselves.

- (incorrect) The three essentials of good manners are: respect, consideration, and understanding. (The words following *are* belong to the statement as its complement.)
- (correct) There are three essentials of good manners: respect, consideration, and understanding.

A Changing Approach to Language

Compare the following two sentences. Each is from page 312 of a novel by a well-known American author, one of the past and one, the present. Each is the opening sentence of its paragraph. First, James Fenimore Cooper, from *The Deerslayer*, written in 1859:

> *As soon as the light was sufficiently strong to allow of a distinct view of the lake, and more particularly of its shores, Hutter turned the head of the ark directly toward the castle, with the avowed intention of taking possession for the day at least, as the place more favorable for meeting his daughters and for carrying on his operations against the Indians.*

Then, Ann Tyler, from *The Accidental Tourist,* written in 1985:

> *He listened for over a minute, and then the call was cut off.*

Picked at random from the works of two widely read American authors, the two sentences show the difference between writers of the past and present. Today's writers use much shorter sentences. The longest sentence written by Tyler on her page 312 has 26 words. Cooper's longest has 64. Cooper's shortest sentence has 17 words. Tyler's shortest sentences have 3 words, and there are five of this length. Tyler's sentences have an average of 8.07 words. Cooper's are almost five times as long, averaging 40.15.

Why are writers like Cooper "hard" to read? Without counting words or syllables, most people would probably guess their difficult vocabularies. Actually, more problems arise from sentence length. That's what really makes the going hard for someone who doesn't understand how grammar works and who gets lost in a long sentence.

Cooper, like all able writers, knows the importance of using shorter words, prepositions, and conjunctions to direct the reader to the strong words—nouns and verbs—that answer the important questions. Yet readers often feel lost because they don't understand how grammar works. Can you spot the main Subject-Verb-Complement of Cooper's 64-word sentence?

- (S-V-C) Hutter/turned/(the) head
    What head? Of the ark
    When? As soon as the light was sufficiently strong
    Where? directly toward the castle
    Why? with the avowed intention of taking possession
    ...and so on.

Here is how someone might rewrite Cooper's sentence today.

Soon the light was sufficiently strong. It allowed a distinct view of the lake. It more particularly gave a good view of its shores. Hutter turned the ark. He headed directly toward the castle. He intended to take possession of it. He meant to hold it for the day at least. It was a place more favorable for meeting his daughter. It was also better for carrying on his operations against the Indians.

Is this an improvement? Using shorter sentences does take a few more words. The important question is, "Does it carry the same meaning?"

In addition to following the rules of grammar, each writer has his own style. In part it's a reflection of his times, and it's also a discovery of his own "voice." At first, a writer's style may seem difficult to read, but after a few paragraphs or pages, you begin to feel the natural rhythm in which he "speaks."

Who is better, Tyler or Cooper? Each has something to say.

TODAY'S PUNCTUATION

Many forms of the written and printed word today borrow from advertising. They contain bold punctuation marks and unusual typographical elements, such as words in italics and all capital letters in order to get as much attention as possible.

How you use punctuation depends largely on what you are writing and who your audience will be. Follow the traditional rules of punctuation for formal writing. It's still important to know the rules—so you will know what effect you want to achieve, when and if you choose to break them.

Chapter 19

How Sentences Combine

I expect a reply.
Two weeks have passed.

Understanding grammar is knowing how parts of sentences fit together. The two short sentences above are simple sentences. They may also be called independent clauses, because they can stand alone. The first has a subject/verb/object. The second has just subject/verb.

One way of joining the two is in a **compound sentence**.

- I expect a reply, and two weeks have passed.

As far as grammar goes, the compound sentence follows a formula.

Two or more   A coordinating
independent +   conjunction   = **a compound sentence**
clauses   to join them

But the fact remains: The two clauses work no better together than they did alone.

COMPLEX SENTENCES

Here are three more versions, combining the same two sentences:

a. I expect a reply because two weeks have passed.
b. I expect a reply although two weeks have passed.
c. I expect a reply after two weeks have passed.

What has happened? One word changes the way the clauses work together. Now, *I expect a reply* has become the more important of the two clauses. The second clause simply answers *Why*, *How*, or *When* about the other's verb, *expect*. It has become an adverb clause, and it's also a dependent clause because of its lesser importance.

An   One or more
independent +   dependent   = **a complex sentence**
clause   clauses

There are three types of dependent clauses, classed by whether they work as adverbs, adjectives, or nouns.

SUBORDINATING CONJUNCTIONS

Conjunctions always count as part of a dependent clause. In a complex sentence, the conjunction is the key. It shows how two clauses are related and how one affects the other's meaning. Don't forget to include the conjunction when identifying a dependent clause.

Conjunctions used in complex sentences are called **subordinating conjunctions** because they place their clause in a position *under* a main clause. *Note*: *subordinate clause* is just another name for *dependent clause*.

ADVERB CLAUSES

Here are words often used as subordinating conjunctions in adverb clauses, along with the questions they most nearly seem to answer.

WHEN?	WHY?	HOW?
after	because	as if
as	if	however
as soon as	in case	provided
before	so that	than
since	unless	
till	although*	WHERE?
until	though*	where
when		wherever
while		

(*in a negative sense)

Don't forget! Many of these words can also work in other ways in a sentence. You must see them in action to be sure.

PRACTICE

Identify the main clause and the dependent clause of each sentence by finding first the S-V-C and then the subordinating conjunction. In **natural order**, as here, the main clause comes first and the subordinating conjunction comes at the place where the two clauses join.

(*Note*: Don't forget that this kind of conjunction is part of its clause because of its importance to the meaning. When an adverb clause follows its main clause in natural order, no comma need separate them.)

1. We have not heard from Chet since he left for Europe.
2. You usually have tattered old magazines to read while you are waiting for an appointment.
3. Fred plays tennis as if he gets plenty of practice.
4. The new system saves time because it combines two steps into one.
5. You usually find a missing object where you put it last.

(For answers, see page 199.)

Punctuating Adverb Clauses

Some adverb clauses can be transposed. When an adverb clause is not in natural order, use a comma between it and the main clause.

Natural Order

- I was in a state of shock after I saw Gina with her new image.

Transposed Order

- After I saw Gina with her new image, I was in a state of shock.

Of course, complex sentences can include more than one adverb clause.

- I have been waiting since the office opened because I have an important question for Mr. Richardson.
- Because I have an important question for Mr. Richardson, I have been waiting since the office opened.

And they can have verbals along with them.

- Coming into the dazzling sunlight, I could not see clearly until my eyes adjusted.
  (S-V) I/could (not) see

The chief requirement of any sentence is a main clause that could stand alone as a sentence. *I could not see* is a perfectly good sentence, all by itself.

Asking the Right Questions

An adverb clause can also modify a verbal working as a noun, adjective, or adverb. Remember, verbals have split personalities—working as various parts of speech, but always keeping some qualities of a verb.

- I wanted to speak with you as soon as you came in.
    (S-V-C) I/wanted/<u>to speak with you</u>
        to speak with you = infinitive phrase
            to speak WHEN?
                <u>as soon as you came in</u>

PRACTICE

First, pick out the S-V-C of the main clause. Next, identify the adverb clause or clauses and the S-V-C of each. Determine what each modifies and what question it answers. Be on the watch for verbals, too.

1. Sandy picked at her eggplant as if she didn't really like it.
2. You can't be sure about a dish until you have tried it.
3. Since squid sounds unappetizing to me, I will only try a small bite of it.
4. Being a very fussy eater, Carol can find little to please her when she eats at fast food restaurants.
5. After you finish, you will enjoy a piece of key lime pie if you have any appetite left.
6. I will meet you wherever you say and whenever the time is convenient for you.
7. We will be working on the project until Monday because many details need testing before the prototype is okayed.

(For answers, see pages 199.)

THE ADJECTIVE CLAUSE

Complex sentences are simply a way of combining ideas. They put sentences together and show what's of greater importance than something else. By using complex sentences, a writer puts ideas in order.

In that way, a complex sentence does more work than a simple sentence. Yet at its heart, there is still a simple, direct thought.

What is the best way to combine the following two sentences?

- Ben is an old friend.
- Ben comes from my hometown, Pittsfield.

None of the adverbial conjunctions fit well, nor would forming a compound sentence help. The key is the word *Ben* used in both sentences.

- Ben is an old friend who comes from my hometown, Pittsfield.

What happens in an adjective clause? The S-V of the second original sentence is

(S-V) Ben/comes

As a dependent clause, it becomes

(S-V) who/comes

In an adjective clause, words such as *who* do double duty. They do not simply join two clauses but take an active part in their own clause. Here, of course, *who* is the subject. Words that work like *who* are called **relative pronouns**.

1. They form an adjective clause by "attaching themselves" or relating to a noun or pronoun in another clause.
2. They also have a definite role to play in their own clause, as subject, direct object, object of a preposition, and so on.

Words commonly used as relative pronouns include

- who, whom   reserved for persons
- which   for animals and things
- that   for persons, animals, and things

There are also compound forms, including *whoever*, *whomever*, and *whichever*. Remember, the same words can do other work in a sentence, such as introduce a question.

Check how the following examples work.

a. The boss liked the suggestion.
   (S-V-C) (The) boss/liked/(the) suggestion

b. Joyce made the suggestion to him.
    (S-V-C) Joyce/made/(the) suggestion

Now combine the two as a complex sentence with adjective clause.

- The boss liked the suggestion that Joyce made to him.

The S-V-C of the dependent clause?

        (S-V-C) Joyce/made/that

That is both direct object and relative pronoun.

    The relative pronoun jumps to the head of the clause to attach itself to the noun which it renames and which the entire adjective clause modifies. *Did you spot the adjective clauses?*

- <u>which</u> it renames
- <u>which</u> the entire adjective clause modifies

Who and Whom

Consider the following:

- Margo is an electrical engineer.
    (S-V-C) Margo/is/(an) engineer
- I recently met Margo.
    (S-V-C) I/met/Margo

This pair of sentences can be combined two ways, depending on which clause you wish to be the main one.

- I recently met Margo, who is an electrical engineer.
- Margo is an electrical engineer whom I met recently.

Why the *whom* in the second example? If you put a pronoun in the place of *Margo*, the reason will be clear.

- She is an electrical engineer.
    She = who, used for relative pronouns in the nominative case
- I recently met her.
    her = whom, for relative pronouns in the objective case

    More of the magic of word order: You can also highlight Margo as an individual, not as the member of a profession.

- Margo, whom I recently met, is an electrical engineer.

Remember that two sentences combined through the use of an adjective clause must both contain the same noun or a noun and its pronoun replacement.

Essential and Nonessential Clauses

- Trent is someone.
- I know him well.

Trent is *someone*? It has a working S-V-C: Trent/is/someone. Yet it sounds incomplete. Then, what about one of these?

- Trent is someone that I know well.
- Trent is someone whom I know well.

As a relative pronoun, *that* should introduce only **essential** adjective clauses. These clauses are necessary to identify or describe a noun in a sentence such as "Trent is someone."

Adjective clauses using *which*, *who*, or *whom* may or may not be essential, depending upon their meaning. If a clause is **nonessential**, use a comma or pair of commas to set it off from the rest of the sentence.

1. Bill Stoddard, who graduated in 1978, holds the school's scoring record.
2. I finally received Jill's letter, which I was awaiting eagerly.
3. We are pleased with the work of Jed McBride, whom Mr. Leland hired last week.

Essential? No commas, please, and, remember *that* in itself says an adjective clause will be essential. Punctuation of other adjective clauses depends on their sense and the writer's intention.

1. A student who graduated in 1981 holds the high jump record.
2. I finally received the letter which Jill promised to write.
3. We are pleased with the work of the man whom Mr. Leland hired.
4. The company and union reached a decision that should satisfy both.

Relative Adverbs

Relative adverbs can also introduce adjective clauses.

- The day when we met was one that I won't forget.
    (S-V-C) (the) day/was/one
    What day? when we met
        (S-V) we/met

When not only modifies *met* but also connects its clause to the subject of the main clause, so that the entire clause modifies the noun, *day*. See the part that word order plays here, too. Relative adverbs and adjectives come at the beginning of an adjective clause. Adjective clauses follow the noun or pronoun they describe.

Here are more words working as relative adverbs.

- The weeks since you left have seemed like years.
- Clark plans to return to Utah, where he was born.
- Older people often love to tell of the days when they were younger.

Notice that adverbs answering *when* and *where* attach adjective clauses to nouns that name *times* and *places*.

Words that can work as relative adverbs include *after*, *before*, *since*, *when*, *where*, *while*, and *why*. When is a word a relative adverb and when a subordinate conjunction? It all depends on what question the clause answers. It *can* be confusing.

- We vacationed at the lake where our friends own a cottage.
  (S-V) We/vacationed
    At *what* lake? where our friends own a cottage—an adjective clause with *where* as a relative adverb
- Some astronauts have gone where no man has ever gone before.
  (S-V) astronauts/have gone
    Have gone *where*? Since the dependent clause answers correctly to *where*, it must be an adverb clause.

It's not a crime that deserves hanging to confuse an adjective clause with an adverb clause. But it is important to identify the main clause and its subject/verb. This is what the sentence is all about. Dependent clauses simply answer questions about the main clause.

Whose: A Relative Adjective

Whose, called a relative adjective, can also introduce an adjective clause.

- I admire the paintings of Monet, whose work is being exhibited at the museum.

Whose modifies *work*; its entire clause modifies *Monet*.

- Nick finally met the composer in whose honor the party was being given.

Whose modifies honor. The party was being given in his (whose) honor. Note that the word order changes and the relative adjective comes after the preposition. This avoids the awkwardness of breaking up the prepositional phrase.

- ■ (awkward) Nick finally met the composer whose honor the party was being given in.

PRACTICE

First, find the main clause and its S-V-C. Then identify the dependent clause and the noun or pronoun that it describes. Decide whether the adjective clause is essential or nonessential.

1. Mark enjoys any kind of music that has a good beat.
2. All of the people whom I asked are in agreement about the new ruling, which recently went into effect.
3. Marian has a new kitten, which she named Beeper.
4. Do you remember the time when you locked yourself out of your apartment?
5. The novel that I just finished will not satisfy anyone who prefers a happy ending.

(For answers, see page 199.)

Combining Sentences

How would you combine each pair of simple sentences into a complex sentence with an adjective clause? With some, there is more than one possibility.

1. The director called extra rehearsals.
   He is a perfectionist.
2. The joke has a punch line.
   I don't understand it.
3. Mr. Carlson is considered an authority on the Civil War.
   Mr. Carlson is a retired army officer.
4. The company president was accused of embezzlement.
   Everyone had trusted the company president.
5. Kent is a natural leader.
   He rarely loses his temper.

(For answers, see page 200.)

Forming Complex Sentences

Once you know how adjective and adverb clauses work, you can put them together and separate them all you wish. The essential ingredient is always a main clause that can stand alone. Then you can add

- one or more adverb clauses
- one or more adjective clauses
- an adjective clause attached to a word in an adjective clause
- verbals

as long as the main clause is clear!

- Before I moved to Michigan, I lived in North Carolina, which is a state that does not have such extreme variations in weather.
    Main clause = I lived in North Carolina
    Adverb clause = Before I moved to Michigan
    Adjective clause = which is a state
    Adjective clause = that does not have such
        extreme variations in weather

Remember, a main clause can sound silly or incomplete when an essential adjective clause is missing.

- Because I was unprepared for Michigan weather, I did not expect summer temperatures that reached 100 degrees and higher.
    (S-V-O) I/did (not) expect/temperatures

This main clause needs its essential adjective clause to sound complete.

PRACTICE

a. Find the main clause and its S-V-C.

b. Identify the dependent clauses.

c. Decide whether the dependent clauses are adjective clauses or adverb clauses by the questions they answer and how they work in the sentence.

1. When we came into the ski lodge, we warmed ourselves by the fireplace.
2. We first attempted the beginners' slope, which seemed high enough to me.
3. Before we left for the ski resort, I bought an outfit that looked perfect for a pro.

4. The moment before I started downhill was a time when I wished to be some-where else.
5. Although I tried not to show it, the instructor recognized someone who was full of panic.
6. When I reached the bottom of the slope, which had seemed so steep, I looked back up toward the top.
7. The slope where I first tried skiing will always be a mountain to me, even though my friends call it a molehill.

(For answers, see page 200.)

To Know What a Word Is, Check to See What It Does

- after
- before
- since
- until

Words such as these can work many ways in sentences: as prepositions, adverbs, subordinate conjunctions, relative adverbs, and even adjectives.

Test yourself on the following "before" and "after" sentences. See if you can tell the difference in their uses. Some are tricky; remember the questions to ask.

1. We left for the airport before dawn.
2. I had never flown by helicopter before.
3. Justine arrived in Washington on the day before the conference officially began.
4. She watched herself on videotape before she felt ready to give her speech at the convention.
5. After the speech there was a question-and-answer period.
6. After the applause ended, Justine was tired but happy.
7. Usually the morning after is unpleasant, but this one spelled relief.

(For answers, see page 200.)

THE NOUN CLAUSE

Who will win?
a. I know the answer.
b. I know who will win.

The noun clause is perhaps the most difficult of dependent clauses. It shows the importance of asking the right question—and believing the answer.

(S-V-C) I/know/_____?_____

Know *what*? In a, it's the noun *answer*. In b, it is *who will win*, which has an (S-V) of its own: who/will win. Like the word *answer*, it is used as the direct object of *know*. As a statement, *who will win* can't stand alone. It is a dependent clause, used as a single part of speech, a **noun clause**, in example b.

Separating a noun clause from its main clause can be tricky because it is often such an important piece of the main clause.

A noun clause can do anything, or almost anything, a noun can.

Subject

- His words puzzled me.
    (S-V-C) words/puzzled/me
- What he said puzzled me.
    (S-V-C) <u>What he said</u>/puzzled/me

Direct Object

- I don't know their address.
- I don't know <u>where they live</u>.

Predicate Nominative

- The choice should be yours.
- The choice should be <u>whichever you like best</u>.

Object of a Preposition

- His appearance was different from my mental image of him.
- His appearance was different from <u>what I imagined</u>.

Object of an Infinitive

- I'd like to understand this computer.
- I'd like to understand <u>how this computer works</u>.

Indirect Object

- You can give visitors the schedule of events.
- You can give <u>whoever wants one</u> the schedule of events.

Retained Object

- I was asked my opinion.
- I was asked <u>what I thought of the President's action</u>.

Appositive

- I will tell you the truth, the plain facts.
- I will tell you the truth, <u>that we are broke</u>.

Noun clauses work like any other words or phrases used as nouns. They answer the noun question, *what*? Noun clauses often express a quality of indefiniteness or doubt. They can also relate to a process. They don't directly answer the question, *Who*?

Words Often Introducing Noun Clauses

Pronouns

> *who, whom, which, what, that,*
> *whoever, whomever, whichever,*
> (Which, what, that, etc., may also be used as adjectives.)

Adverbs

> *how, where, why, if, whether, when*

A Conjunction

> *that* (sometimes used merely to "join" a noun clause to the rest of its sentence.)

- I know that you are right.
  (S-V-C) I/know/that you are right

Note: *That* is often left out and understood.

- I know you are right.
  (S-V-C) I/know/(that) you are right

Why Are Noun Clauses Difficult?

A noun clause is almost always part of the main clause, which usually doesn't make complete sense without it. A noun clause can even belong to the heart of a main clause and be its subject or complement. A noun clause has a subject and verb of its own. The connecting word may or may not be part of it.

Working with Noun Clauses

Begin with a simple sentence.

- I know your name.
  (S-V-C) I/know/name

Turn it into a complex sentence that contains a noun clause.

a. I know what you want.
   (S-V-C) I/know/<u>what you want</u>
      (Noun clause S-V-C) you/want/what
      what is a direct object in its clause
b. I know why you came.
   (Noun clause S-V) you/came
   why is an adverb in its clause
c. I know who you are.
   (Noun clause S-V-C) you/are/who
   who is a predicate nominative in its clause
d. I know whom you saw.
   (Noun clause S-V-C) you/saw/whom
   whom is the direct object of *saw*
e. I know that can't be true.
   (Noun clause S-V-C) that/can (not) be/true
   that is the subject in the noun clause
f. I know that story is true.
   story is the subject; *that*, its adjective
g. I know that it is true.
   (Noun clause S-V-C) it/is/true
   that is a conjunction; you could just as well say, "I know it is true."

To know how noun clauses work, as with everything in grammar, you just need to ask the right question.

In complex sentences, noun clauses often work to allow the delay or qualification of a piece of information. In the examples, note how both sentences are introduced by observations concerning the statements made in the noun clauses.

Examples

- It is amazing how fast gossip travels.
   (S-V-C) <u>how fast gossip travels</u>/is/amazing
      it = an introductory word, an expletive
      The noun clause is the true subject.
- I don't know why Charley didn't tell me first.
   (S-V-C) I/do(n't) know/<u>why Charley didn't tell me first</u>

Noun Clauses in Questions

Remember, questions are often in transposed order. This is especially true of questions with noun clauses.

- Who do you think is most talented?
    (S-V-C) You/do think/<u>who is most talented</u>
    (Noun clause S-V) who/is/talented
- Whom do you think he will choose?
    (S-V-C) you/do think/<u>he/will choose/whom</u>

To be "right" in grammar, choose a pronoun because of its actual work in its own clause, not from its place at the beginning of a sentence. In speaking, it's sometimes hard to know at the beginning of a sentence exactly where it will end. But in writing, always check to make sure what pronouns such as *I/me, she/her, he/him, we/us, they/them,* and *who/whom* really do. It's another "fine" point of good grammar.

PRACTICE

First, spot the main S-V-C. Remember that a noun clause can work as the subject or complement of the main clause. Decide how each noun clause is used in its sentence. Watch for a sentence having more than one noun clause.

1. I understand why Hubie felt embarrassed.
2. Whoever calls can leave a message on the answering machine.
3. Some people never want what is best for them.
4. Your birthday cake will be whatever flavor you like.
5. I have been thinking about what you told me.
6. Tell whomever you call how important the meeting is.
7. Where he has gone is anyone's guess.

(For answers, see page 200.)

Chapter 20

Keeping It Simple, Even When Sentences Get Complex

Remember how it began?

A Simple Sentence:
  The family spent its vacation in Rome.
A Simple Sentence with Compound Predicate:
  They enjoyed the sights and loved the Italian people.
A Compound Sentence:
  Pasta is the order of the day, and Italians know countless ways to make it.
A Complex Sentence:
  If you go to Italy, you should leave all thoughts of dieting behind.
And even a Compound-Complex Sentence:
  When you come home, you can show people your souvenirs and photos, but nothing compares with actually being there.
Verbals: Infinitives, Gerunds, and Participles . . .

In the real world of using English, you can put them together and scramble them up in endless combinations.

WHAT "GOOD" IS A COMPLEX SENTENCE?

English is basically a word-order language. A simple sentence states a simple, direct thought.

- Baby wants a cookie.

A verbal adds a new idea.

- Baby wants mother to bring him a cookie.

A dependent clause adds another.

- Baby wants mother to bring him one of the chocolate cookies that she bought at the supermarket yesterday.

And there's another half to the situation that will make the sentence compound.

- Baby wants mother to bring him one of the chocolate cookies that she bought at the supermarket yesterday, or Baby will cry.

Why? One more dependent clause will explain.

- Baby wants mother to bring him one of the chocolate cookies that she bought at the supermarket yesterday, or Baby will cry because that usually gets results fast.

Is a complex sentence better than a simple sentence? It all depends. It depends upon what needs to be said.

In many ways a complex sentence does more work than a simple one. It organizes ideas and ties them together. It can show what is more important than something else. It can show cause and effect because it makes clear how one thing depends upon another.

A complex sentence can sometimes make life easier because it can show the relative importance of clauses and thereby help clarify a complicated idea. But beware of someone who uses fancy grammar just to impress and to dress up a dull, unoriginal idea; it happens more often than you might think.

A simple idea often requires a simple sentence; a complex idea, a complex one.

THE SOUND OF LANGUAGE

Good writers know that language also contains sound and rhythm. This also is a part of seeing how grammar and word order work. A good writer knows that verbals and dependent clauses and joining words carry the reader along. They make the key words, the nouns and verbs, "ring out" and become more important.

Writer at Work

Following is a new, rewritten version, revised into simple sentences, of two paragraphs from F. Scott Fitzgerald's *The Great Gatsby*. They describe a fabulous party taking place at Gatsby's mansion during Prohibition, the Jazz Age.

> *By seven o'clock the orchestra has arrived. It is no thin five-piece affair. There is a whole pitful of oboes, trombones, saxophones, viols, cornets, piccolos, and low and high drums. The last swimmers have come in from the beach now. They are dressing upstairs. The cars from New York are parked five deep in the drive. Already the halls, salons, and verandas are gaudy with primary colors. Girls wear their hair shorn in strange new ways. Their shawls are colorful beyond the dreams of Castile. The bar is in full swing. Floating rounds of cocktails permeate the garden outside. The air is alive with chatter, laughter, casual innuendo, and introductions. They are all forgotten on the spot. There are enthusiastic meetings between women. They never even knew each other's names.*

> *The lights grow brighter. The earth lurches away from the sun. Now the orchestra is playing yellow cocktail music. The opera of voices pitches a key higher. Laughter is easier minute by minute. It is spilled with prodigality. It is tipped out at a cheerful word. The groups change more swiftly. They swell with new arrivals. They dissolve and form in the same breath. Already there are wanderers. Confident girls weave here and there among the stouter and more stable. They become for a sharp, joyous moment the center of a group. Then they become excited with triumph. They glide on through the sea-change of faces, voices, and color. The light also is constantly changing.*

Does F. Scott Fitzgerald Do It Better?

Now see how Fitzgerald uses not only phrases and clauses but also words like *and* to bring the picture of the party together. Compare how the simple sentences fit within his longer ones. By knowing how grammar works, Fitzgerald makes his sentences also carry the idea of combining and changing and movement that the people at the party engaged in.

> *By seven o'clock the orchestra has arrived, no thin five-piece affair, but a whole pitful of oboes and trombones and saxophones and viols and cornets and piccolos, and low and high drums. The last swimmers have come in from the beach now and are dressing upstairs; the cars from New York are parked five deep in the drive, and already the halls and salons and verandas are gaudy with primary colors, and hair shorn in*

strange new ways, and shawls beyond the dreams of Castile. The bar is in full swing, and floating rounds of cocktails permeate the garden outside, until the air is alive with chatter and laughter, and casual innuendo and introductions forgotten on the spot, and enthusiastic meetings between women who never knew each other's names.

The lights grow brighter as the earth lurches away from the sun, and now the orchestra is playing yellow cocktail music, and the opera of voices pitches a key higher. Laughter is easier minute by minute, spilled with prodigality, tipped out at a cheerful word. The groups change more swiftly, swell with new arrivals, dissolve and form in the same breath; already there are wanderers, confident girls who weave here and there among the stouter and more stable, become for a sharp, joyous moment the center of a group, and then, excited with triumph, glide on through the sea-change of faces and voices and color under the constantly changing light.

To be good with language, you need an ear for its music as well as a knowledge of its rules of grammar. Good grammar and good writing are not the same thing.

GRAMMAR IN ACTION

A real writer will create sentences that may be difficult to analyze. When you read, try to be aware of the simple sentences that lie under the more complex forms. You do not need to know exactly how every word and phrase works, just as you do not need to know the meaning of every word in order to benefit from what you read.

Keep in mind the simple sentences that Charles Dickens combines to create this picture of an English town he calls Coketown. It is from his novel *Hard Times*, in which a school master called Gradgrind claims, "In this life, we want nothing but Facts, sir; nothing but Facts."

Coketown, a city dedicated to facts, is as dull as its school.

It was a town of red brick, or of brick that would have been red if the smoke and ashes had allowed it; but as matters stood it was a town of unnatural red and black like the painted face of a savage. It was a town of machinery and tall chimneys, out of which interminable serpents of smoke trailed themselves forever and ever, and never got uncoiled. It had a black canal in it, and a river that ran purple with ill-smelling dye, and vast piles of buildings full of windows where there was a rattling and trembling all day long, and where the piston of the steam-engine worked monotonously up and down like the head of an elephant in a state of melancholy madness. It contained several large streets all very like one another, and many small streets still more like one another, inhabited by people equally like one another, who all went in and out at the same hours, with the same sound upon the same pavements, to do the same work, and to whom every day was the same as yesterday and tomorrow, and every year the counterpart of the last and the next.

. . . You saw nothing in Coketown but what was severely workful.

Can you find the simple sentences that join together to form the compound and complex ones? Did you notice repeated words, such as *like*, with which Dickens calls attention to what he considers important?

A sentence can be as long or as short as it needs to be. The only requirement is that its parts join together and depend upon one another clearly and correctly. It can never be too short or too long if it says what it needs to say.

WHAT MAKES GRAMMAR IMPORTANT?

Here's what Robert Claiborne writes in *Our Marvelous Native Tongue*. Read it both for ideas and for an understanding of how another writer combines sentences.

If, in 1700, you were chatting with another resident of your native town or village, understanding was no problem: both of you would almost certainly use the same syntax, acquired in childhood, and any unclarity of meaning could be quickly resolved by asking, "What do you mean?" The writer preparing his copy for the printer was in quite a different situation: he was addressing himself to people he had never seen and in all likelihood never would see. If they found his syntax obscure, they could not cross-question him, but would likely damn him for an ignoramus and resolve never to read him again.

And, on the same subject, Daniel J. Boorstin writes in *The Discoverers*:

After Gutenberg (1454), realms of everyday life once ruled and served by Memory would be governed by the printed page. In the late Middle Ages, for the small literate class, manuscript books had provided an aid, and sometimes a substitute, for Memory. But the printed book was far more portable, more accurate, more convenient to refer to, and of course, more public. Whatever was in print, after being written by an author, was also known to printers, proofreaders, and anyone reached by the printed page. A man could now refer to the rules of grammar. . . .

Whether writing about grammar or expertly using it, these writers show the true importance of knowing how grammar works.

WHAT MAKES GRAMMAR IMPORTANT?

Chapter 21

Verbs Do More:
The Fine Points
of Using Verbs

Working with verbs proves that verbs do more than express the idea of an action or the act of being. Verbs never just lie there; they always take an active part in a sentence.

1. Verbs express time or tense, such as

Present	Past
I see	I saw

2. Verbs also have voice.

Active	Passive
I see	I was seen

3. Verbs may change to express number.

Third Person Singular	Others
She (he, it) sees.	They see.

4. Verbs may act on objects or act alone. Some work both ways.

Intransitive	Transitive
We see.	We see someone.

5. Verbs help direct the purpose of a sentence.

Statement	Question
You see.	Do you see?

Command	Exclamation
See.	How you see!

VERBS HAVE THEIR MOODS

In grammar, there's no such thing as a "good" or "bad" mood. **Mood** simply means the attitude of the speaker toward the words spoken. English has three moods: *indicative*, *imperative*, and *subjunctive*. You've already seen two of them at work to help indicate a speaker's purpose.

Indicative

In any tense or voice, **indicative** is the mood that shows or points out that the verb is simply dealing with actual data. Most statements, questions, and exclamations use the indicative mood.

- Do you like horror movies?
- I enjoy them very much.

Obviously, those are indicative.

- A three-headed monster ate my brother-in-law.
- What a struggle that must have been!

Those, too, are indicative. The indicative mood does not mean a sentence must be taken seriously. It means that its chief aim is simply to convey its meaning. It is the mood used for the ordinary expression of most statements and questions.

Imperative

The **imperative** mood is used for giving commands.

- Listen here.
- Be happy.
- Don't waste a second!
- Try to be both strong and gentle, firm and loving.

The imperative is the base form of the verb used with a "you understood" subject. It expresses an order or direct request to do as the speaker commands.

Subjunctive

- How I wish I were back home!

(I am, I was, I will be, I . . .)

But "I were" is never right.

(We were, you were, they were, never "I were.")

Yet that's how the subjunctive mood works. It uses an out-of-the-ordinary verb form to call attention to the fact that it's saying something unusual.

To signal that the subjunctive is at work, these are the basic changes:

- <u>was</u> to <u>were</u>
- <u>am</u>, <u>is</u>, <u>are</u>, to <u>be</u>
- dropping the final s from the -s form the third person singular (she <u>sees</u> to she <u>see</u>).

Like many other precise old forms of language, the subjunctive is also disappearing from use. One reason is that English uses different helpers, instead of making actual changes in the verb itself. This can achieve a similar effect without truly being the subjunctive. But many people who care about language are still listening, and paying attention to the subjunctive is another way to show respect for the tools of language.

Here's where and how the subjunctive still makes a difference.

1. *It expresses a condition contrary to fact.* Compare the following sentences:

   a. If I were a big lottery winner, I would quit working.
   b. If I win the lottery, I will quit working.
   c. I was a big lottery winner, so I quit working.

Of course, example a illustrates the subjunctive in action.
The word *subjunctive* also contains the idea of being "under" another idea. Here it's usually in a dependent clause that answers the question *why*: if something contrary to fact took place. Notice how the main clause of example a uses the helping verb *would*, which also shows it's just a possibility.
Both b and c are in the indicative mood. Example c shows how "was" expresses a fact, in contrast to the condition contrary to fact in example a.
    All three of the following dependent clauses are in the subjunctive mood.

- Mike would have more friends if he were not so conceited.
- If I were taller, this dress might look better.
- I you were I, what would you do?

Notice that "you were" is no different from the indicative form. Along with "they," "we," and other plural nouns and pronouns, its verb doesn't change in the subjunctive. One reason the subjunctive is disappearing is that it's not always evident. Sometimes you must simply know it's there.

2. *Subjunctive expresses a neutral condition or strong doubt.*

- If the rumor were true, what could we do to help?
- If there be any justice, we will win the case.
- I enjoy all kinds of good music, whether it be classical or modern, symphonic or jazz.

3. *The subjunctive is used in noun clauses after wishes, orders, strong requests.*

- I wish California weren't so far away from New York.
- I demanded that he give me the money.
- Her parents forbid that she see him again.
- I insist that you be quiet.

4. *The subjunctive is used in a separate clause to express a deep desire.*

- If only Ted were here!
- Would I were wrong!
- Heaven help us!
- If I had only listened!

Note: Sometimes an *if* clause expresses a fact that the speaker hadn't known beforehand. In this case, the indicative mood is used.

- If Edie was home, why didn't she answer the phone?

PRACTICE

In the following sentences, choose the word that properly expresses the subjunctive mood.

1. If there _____ more time, we could stop and see Maxie. (was, were)
2. The director insists that everyone _____ on time for rehearsal. (be, is)
3. He tried to act as though he _____ not hurt by the thoughtless remark. (was, were)
4. Mr. Smith demanded that Tom _____ until the work was finished. (stay, stays)
5. I wish that Alex _____ here. (was, were)

6. The boss asks that the receptionist _____ all callers by their first names. (addresses, address)

7. If someone _____ to ask, I'd tell them that I think this project is a waste of time. (was, were)

(For answers, see page 200.)

COMMON VERBS THAT CAUSE GREAT CONFUSION

Some of the most common verbs have sound-alike forms that are also close in meaning but have important differences in their proper usage.

They are so often confused that only thought, practice, and careful listening will keep them separated. In each case, the difference is based on how they work in sentences—whether they are are transitive (in need of an object) or intransitive (not in need of one).

Transitive*	Intransitive
lay	lie
(laid, laid, laying)	(lay, lain, lying)
set	sit
(set, set, setting)	(sat, sat, sitting)
raise	rise
(raised, raised, raising)	(rose, risen, rising)

*With only a very few exceptions

Is it rise or raise? Sit or set? Lie or lay? And how dare one *lay* be the past tense of *lie*, while the other has *lay*, *laid*, and *laid* as its principal parts? No wonder it's confusing—and a tricky test of someone's skill in usage.

Think of them as the transitive trio: lay, set, raise.

- I usually <u>lay</u> my sunglasses in the same place.
  (I <u>put</u> my sunglasses there.)
- I <u>set</u> the highchair in the corner, and then I <u>set</u> the baby in it.
  (I <u>put</u> the highchair in the corner, and then I <u>put</u> the baby in it.)
- I <u>raised</u> my hand.
  (I <u>put up</u> my hand.)

A reasonable test for *lay*, *set*, and *raise* is to put a form of *put* in its place. If it makes sense, you're right.

Compare them with the intransitive trio: lie, sit, rise. Remember, things can lie, sit, and rise as well as people.

- I <u>lie</u> in bed late on Saturday morning.
- A gum wrapper <u>lies</u> on the sidewalk.
- Gramps always <u>sits</u> in the same chair.
- The clock <u>sits</u> on the shelf.
  (Think of them all as just "resting" there.)
- Gramps always <u>rises</u> at 6 A.M., no matter when the sun <u>rises</u>.
  (<u>Rise</u> means to get or go up.)

PRACTICE

The Transitive Trio

In the following sentences, pick out the subject/verb/complement. Be sure to include helping verbs. Know the tense of each verb and its voice, active or passive. Remember, a verb that can be transitive is necessary to form the passive voice.

1. We have set our hopes on a victory.
2. The fans in the stands raised their voices and sang the school song.
3. The referee laid the ball on the one yard line.
4. With one more touchdown pass, the quarterback will set a school scoring record.
5. Our spirits were raised by the halftime score.
6. The coach is laying the groundwork for a surprise play.
7. Tomorrow, we will raise the victory banner to the top of the campus flagpole.

(For answers, see page 200.)

The Intransitive Trio

For each clause, find the subject/verb. Being intransitive, none of the verbs will have a complement. Decide the tense of each verb, and pay attention to how the meaning determines its choice. Watch for compound and complex sentences.

1. All morning long a fog lay over the countryside.
2. Although the sun had risen, ghostly blobs of mist were still sitting close to the ground.
3. A dog was lying in the yard.
4. The farmer usually rose with the sun.
5. An old, fallen tree trunk had lain across the creek for years.

6. Two boys sat on it, fishing, and another lay stretched out on his back.
7. The water level was rising because of the recent rains.

(For answers, see page 201.)

All Six Together

In the following sentences, first identify the subjects, along with any helping verbs and objects. Next, choose the correct base form of the verb from the pair in parentheses. Then fill in the blank with the principal part of this verb that fits both tense and meaning. If in doubt, check the chart on page 155 giving the principal parts of each verb.

1. Jody Anderson has _____ to the top of his profession. (raise, rise)
2. The spices have _____ too long on the kitchen shelf. (set, sit)
3. Stu has _____ on the beach under the blazing sun for hours. (lay, lie)
4. Construction prices have been _____ in the suburban area. (raise, rise)
5. Will you _____ the report on top of that stack of papers? (set, sit)
6. Many papers were _____ in a jumble on the desk. (lay, lie)
7. Money for the team's new uniforms was _____ by the Boosters Club. (raise, rise)
8. On sleepless nights I have _____ awake for hours, listening to murmuring motors. (lay, lie)
9. The owners have _____ rust-colored outdoor carpet on their patio. (lay, lie)
10. The company president will _____ for a portrait. (set, sit)

(For answers, see page 201.)

More Common "Problem" Verbs

go   went, gone, going
do   did, done, doing
see   saw, seen, seeing
run   ran, run, running
come   came, come, coming

What's the problem? It's really usage, not grammar. How do you choose the right principal part? To be sure, you need to understand how verbs work and to recognize the perfect tenses and passive voice.

As you fill in the blanks in the following exercise, be sure to check for either helpers (has, have, had, will have) that signal a perfect tense or a form of *be* that marks the passive voice. Either calls for the third principal part of the verb.

1. I would not have _____ without you. (go, went, gone)
2. Whatever Althea _____, she _____ well. (do, did, done)
3. As soon as Benny saw them coming, he _____ to tell his mother. (run, ran, run)
4. I had never _____ so far or so fast in my life. (run, ran, run)
5. Sara told us that she _____ everything that happened. (see, saw, seen)
6. We were glad to know Harvey had _____ back. (come, came, come)
7. At last night's party, most people _____ straight from work. (come, came, come)

(For answers, see page 201.)

Don't forget the difference between *do* and *does*, *don't* and *doesn't*.

- We don't smoke, he does.
- We do care, he doesn't.

Little Words That Count a Lot

not	never	barely
hardly	scarcely	almost

- The program has begun.
    (S-V) (The) program/has begun
  The program has not begun.
  The program has barely begun.
  The program has only just begun.
  The program has almost begun.
- I can understand you.
    (S-V-C) I/can understand/you
  I cannot understand you.
  I can never understand you.
  I can hardly ever understand you.
  I can scarcely understand you.
  I can't understand you.

These little words seem to be adverbs in the truest sense of the word. They never count as part of the verb itself. Yet they work closely with it and turn its meaning this way and that.

As an adverb, *not* can even attach itself in a contraction to the end of a verb, as in *can't, couldn't, shouldn't, wouldn't, mustn't, isn't, aren't, wasn't, weren't, don't, doesn't, didn't, hasn't, haven't,* and *hadn't.* The shortened forms simply add *n't,* for not, to their regular form except for *won't* (will not) and, now rarely used, *shan't* (shall not). Even attached, the *n't* isn't really part of the verb. It's still an adverb.

What's the difference?

> It isn't formal.
> and
> It is not formal.

If you want to be formal in speech or writing, contractions aren't. Writing out *not* makes the negative turn sound more emphatic, too.

Here are some other words that strike a negative note.

> I have <u>no</u> money.
> I saw <u>none</u> of my friends.
> You understand <u>nothing</u>.
> I met <u>nobody</u>.

ONE NEGATIVE IS ENOUGH

A double negative makes you sound illiterate. People who hear mistakes in grammar always catch a double negative. To their ears, it actually sounds painful, for it's one of the "worst" errors you can make. *It might even get you thrown right out of the ball park.*

Error
> The Tigers didn't allow no base hits.

Error free
> The Tigers didn't allow any base hits.
> The Tigers allowed no base hits.

Error
> I hadn't never seen a major league game before.

Error free
> I had never seen a major league game before.
> I hadn't ever seen a major league game before.

Error
> You can't hardly tell the difference.

Error free
> You can hardly tell the difference.

It's easy to correct a double negative. Just get rid of either one and keep the other.

BE CAREFUL OF "OF"

- You would have liked the concert.
  (S-V-C) You/would have liked/(the) concert
- You would of liked the concert.

What's the *of* doing? Where does it come from? Maybe it sounds like *'ve*, a contraction for have, as in *You should've been there*.

Should of, could of, ought to of, might of, would of—some even seem to think it's shoulda, coulda, mighta, woulda. When you know how grammar works, you would have, ought to have, might have, must have, and definitely should have known that *of* should have been *have*.

PRACTICE

Each of these sentences contains one or more errors likely to be made only by someone who doesn't understand how grammar works. Identify and correct them.

1. I didn't mean to insult nobody.
2. It don't matter to me.
3. Hank could have went back to work.
4. I come right after you called.
5. If I was you, I wouldn't tell nobody what I done.
6. The old dog would of laid there all day.
7. There wasn't nobody setting in the front row.
8. The neighbors done all they could of to help.
9. We never had no doubt that we seen a genius at work.
10. When Monday come, we would of welcomed another weekend.

(For answers, see page 201.)

SPLITTING INFINITIVES

In English, infinitives are usually two words: *to* + the base of the verb (to go, to be, to come, to make, to see). In Latin, an infinitive is only one word, and so it is impossible to split. So who cares whether you split an infinitive? Many grammar experts say it doesn't matter; fussy folks still say it does.

If you have *to* really *work* at splitting an infinitive, don't.

If an unsplit infinitive seems to really destroy the balance of a sentence, go ahead and split it.

Did you spot the two split infinitives in the last two sentences? Are they necessary? Here are more examples.

- *split:* It is time <u>to</u> actually <u>begin</u> working on the project, not <u>to</u> just <u>talk</u> about it.
- *whole:* It is time actually <u>to begin</u> working on the project, not just <u>to talk</u> about it.

Positioning Adverbs

According to the workings of word order, it's often possible to move an adverb and not greatly change the meaning. For example:

- The millionaire gives generously to worthy causes.
- The millionaire generously gives to worthy causes.
- The millionaire gives to worthy causes generously.

But what of the following?

- I try never to be thoughtless.
- I never try to be thoughtless. (I just am?)
- I try to never be thoughtless. (Does splitting *to be* help?)

There are still people listening who don't like the sound of a split infinitive.

MAKING PERFECT USE OF THE PERFECT TENSES

The perfect tenses give an idea of completion.

1. Combine the *past perfect* with a *simple past* to show the first was completed before the second.

   - Jake <u>had</u> already <u>gone</u> when we <u>arrived</u>.
   - Kim <u>had known</u> about the meeting before I <u>told</u> her.

2. The *future perfect* speaks of a future event to take place before another future event.

- I <u>will have forgotten</u> all my French by the time I have a chance to go to Paris.
- Someone else <u>will have pointed</u> out the mistake before I do.

3. The *present perfect* can be used alone and also works with present, past, future, or another present perfect tense.

- You <u>have explained</u> the situation perfectly.
- I am sure that Al <u>has gone</u>.
- Val's work shows that she <u>has studied</u> a great deal.

In writing a paper, avoid switching back and forth in tenses. Choose the present or past, and stay with it unless there is dialogue or another good reason to change. Here is a bad example. Identify the verbs in it. Then make the correct choices in either all present or all past tense.

> In the novel, the heroine was born in London. She grows up in an orphanage. Then she is adopted by a wealthy family. After they took her to live on their country estate, her life becomes very different. A rich nobleman fell in love with her, but she marries his penniless brother.

Chapter 22

Questions of Usage: How Can Words Agree with One Another when People Don't Agree?

Which of the following is correct?

a. Everyone has his own opinion.
b. Everyone has their own opinion.
c. Everyone has his or her own opinion.

One thing is sure. *Everyone* has an opinion. An oldtime schoolmaster would have no problem drilling his pupils on the right answer. "Definitely," he would say, "it is *his*." He had excellent reasons for being sure his version was right, and many of those on the lookout for "mistakes in grammar" would still agree.

Does it really matter? In a time when everyone seems to be taking sides, it does matter to many.

"*His* opinion?" exclaim the feminists. "What about *her*?" Their vote goes to c, with *his or her*, just as they believe in replacing *salesman* with *salesperson* and *chairman* with *chairperson*, to get rid of sexist overtones.

What about *their*? It may be the choice of someone who just doesn't know better. Or someone who wants to avoid taking sides. Or could it even be someone who doesn't count?

In some ways, grammar is more than how language works. It also expresses how people think and feel. For that reason, it's both what you say and how you say it that tell the entire story.

INDEFINITE PRONOUNS AND NOUNS

The Singular Indefinites

If you can remember one key indefinite pronoun, the rest come easily. Then, just take *every-*, *any-*, *no-* and *some-* and pair them with *-one*, *-body*, and *-thing* in every way you can: *everyone*, *no one*, *someone*, *somebody*, *everybody*, *nobody*, *nothing*, *something*, *everything*, *anything*, *anybody*, *anyone*, and so on. And using the same idea, *each*, *either*, *neither*, *another*, *one*. It's easy to name more than a dozen by starting with one.

Compare the following sentences.

- Chuck is coming.
- Lynn is coming.
- Everyone is coming.

Or, if the worst happens,

- No one is coming.

It's not hard to agree that each of these indefinite pronouns needs a singular verb, such as *was*, *has*, *does*, or *wants*.

Now compare this set of sentences.

- Chuck has lost his jacket.
- Lynn has lost her jacket.
- Somebody has lost _____.

Here's where the trouble comes in today.

The schoolmaster would say, "Somebody has lost his jacket." Both *somebody* and *has* are singular. Obviously, the possessive adjective should agree. "Sexist! It should be 'Somebody has lost his or her jacket,'" cries the crusader who also knows grammar. "Too awkward," comes the reply. "Besides, *he* and *his* are merely pronouns. They are simply words and have always been used indefinitely to mean either sex." Who's right? In questions of grammar, logic doesn't necessarily win out. If you don't believe that, just look at that illogical word, *be*.

Some Indefinite Guidelines

- Everyone has their own opinion.
  Their is "wrong." But doesn't it solve the sexism problem nicely?
- Everyone has his own opinion.
  If you want your armor to be the old rules of grammar, carry on the fight.
- Everyone has his or her own opinion.
  It is awkward, isn't it? And shouldn't it be "her or his?"

You can usually avoid the situation entirely.

- Everyone is entitled to an opinion.
- Someone has lost a jacket.
- You have your own opinion, just as everyone else has.

Whatever you choose, prepare to defend yourself.

Indefinite Plurals: No Problem

Indefinite pronouns such as *everyone* and *each* single out one of a group and use it to stand for the rest. Four are strictly plural: *both, few, many,* and *several.* They are always in agreement with plural verbs, possessives, and other pronouns.

- Both of the plans have their good points.
- Few of the children's toys are ever as durable as they are advertised to be.
- Several of the guests have expressed their thanks.
- Many of the styles are still on sale.

Some Indefinite Pronouns That Go Either Way

- *Most* of the seats have been filled.
- *Most* of the room has been repainted.

Certain indefinite pronouns work with either singular or plural, depending upon whether they deal with numbers or quantity.

The Truly Indefinite of Indefinite Pronouns
(May be singular or plural)

all	most
any	none
enough	plenty
more	some

How do you know whether their use is singular or plural? Just check to see what they refer to.

- Chocolate cake?
  Enough is left for dinner.
- Eggs?
  Enough are left for omelettes.
- An insult?
  All is forgiven.
- Debts?
  All are paid.

If the pronoun in question deals with a number of items that can be counted, use the plural. If a quantity, unit, or quality, use the singular.

- Some of the grains were impossible to pick up.
- Some of the sugar has spilled on the floor.

None also works either way, according to its intended effect.

- None of my suggestions were taken.
- None of us is ready to give the presentation.

Much, *little*, and *less* are used indefinitely *only* in matters of quantity or portion.

- Less was said about the problem than I expected.
- Little is known.
- Much is hoped.

What Is the Subject?

Many of the indefinite pronouns also work as adjectives. The difference can be important in matters of agreement. *Usage*, or using words in a certain way, becomes a matter of habit. When there's doubt, knowing how a word works can help you make the right choice.

Compare the following sentences.

- Each of the cereal boxes was almost empty.
  (S-V-C) each/was/empty
- Each question deserves a thoughtful answer.
  (S-V-C) question/deserves/answer
- One of the large suitcases has wheels.
  (S-V-C) One/has/wheels
- Some suitcases have wheels.
  (S-V-C) suitcases/have/wheels

Remember, it is the subject that controls the verb, not an adjective or an object of a preposition.

- One of the letters that are on today's editorial page is mine.
  (S-V-C) one/is/mine
    What one? <u>of the letters</u>, an adjective prepositional phrase
    What letters? <u>that are on today's editorial page</u>, an adjective clause
    modifying *letters*
      (S-V) that/are

Note: *That* is used here as a relative pronoun. Its verb depends on the word it's attached to. Since *letters* is plural, it needs the plural verb *are*.

Here is another point of agreement.

- There is plenty of time.
  (S-V) plenty/is
- There are plenty of potato chips.
  (S-V) plenty/are

There is often an introductory word, an expletive, or in some sentences, an adverb. It is not the subject.

Always be sure to check for the real subject, whether or not *there* is used along with an indefinite pronoun.

DEMONSTRATIVE PRONOUNS AND ADJECTIVES

	Near	*Not so near*
Singular	this	that
Plural	these	those

This is my popcorn. That is his. These are my pretzels. Those are yours. This Coke is mine. That Pepsi is yours. These tapes and those albums are my favorites. *This* and *these* carry a sense of being "here," while *that* and *those* imply being "there." For this reason, it's unnecessary and is even thought illiterate to include the adverbs in such sentences as:

- (ouch!) This here is my bowl of popcorn, and that there is yours.
- (ouch!) I'd like one of them there candy bars.

Don't use *them*, a pronoun, with *there* as a pointer. One word does the job.

- I'd like one of those candy bars, please.

PRACTICE

Check the subject-verb of each sentence and clause. Then pick the word in parentheses that agrees with the indefinite pronoun or subject noun controlling the correct choice.

1. Everybody in the cast _____ (is, are) ready for opening night but Neil.
2. Each of the cars _____ (has, have) good qualities of _____ (its, their) own.
3. Most of Ruben Blades's hits _____ (is, are) in Spanish.
4. _____ (Is, Are) any of the airlines offering a special fare to Florida?
5. More paint _____ (is, are) needed to finish the job.
6. Most of the cans _____ (is, are) empty.
7. Fewer people _____ (is, are) coming this year; less food _____ (is, are) needed.
8. Each of the novels that _____ (is, are) on the reading list _____ (was, were) written by a different author.
9. There _____ (is, are) much of the work still undone.
10. There _____ (is, are) one of the many problems that _____ (is, are) waiting to be solved.

(For answers, see page 201.)

COMPOUND PERSONAL PRONOUNS

Person	Singular	Plural
1st	myself	ourselves
2nd	yourself	yourselves
3rd	herself, himself, itself	themselves

Use the compound form of a personal pronoun when its simple form or the noun it names is in the same sentence. There are three correct ways to use a compound personal pronoun.

1. When it is acted upon by itself—this is called the **reflexive** use.

- I asked myself what went wrong.
- He cut himself on the can lid.
- Save a piece of cake for yourself.
  (S-V-C?) *You* is the understood subject
- You will do yourselves a favor by listening carefully.

2. When it is repeated for emphasis—this is called the **intensive** use.

- They themselves accept the full responsibility.
- It is a decision that only she herself can make.
- I know what I myself would do in that case.

3. When it acts as a predicate nominative.

- Mitzi has not been herself recently.
- After a rest, he became himself again.

Warning: Do not use the compound personal pronoun if it doesn't relate to another pronoun or noun in the same sentence.

- (ouch!) From myself and my associates, you can expect complete cooperation.
- (ouch!) It is people like yourself that make this company a success.
- (ouch!) My fiancee and myself wish to thank you.

Sentences like these are sometimes affected as examples of high-class grammar. They are, simply, wrong. It is better to say,

- You can be sure of our complete cooperation.
- It is people like you that make this company a success.
- My fiancee and I wish to thank you.

Theirselves and *hisself* aren't accepted as compound personal pronouns.

- (ouch!) People should take good care of theirselves by exercising and watching their diets.
- (ouch!) Did you hear what he bought hisself?

It's correct to say

- People should take good care of themselves.
- Did you hear what he bought himself?

AGREEMENT BETWEEN SUBJECT AND VERB

The General Rule: A verb agrees with its subject in person and number.

> Most nouns form their plurals by adding -s or -es. The dictionary shows exceptions.
> A singular noun takes a present tense verb that ends in -s. Note that a final s is usually the sign of plural for nouns but of singular present for verbs.

- This photograph seems out of focus.
- These photographs seem out of focus.

With the majority of nouns and pronouns, making subjects and verbs agree is a matter of logic. First of all, you must be able to identify the subject, and that's where understanding grammar comes in.

In some cases, the correct choice is governed by usage, which is based upon custom. The questions of agreement discussed below include some of the most troublesome exceptions. Because usage deals with individual words, not the system of grammar itself, check a dictionary when you're in doubt.

Nouns That Act as Exceptions

1. Some nouns are commonly used with singular verbs although plural in form.

- news, politics, economics, athletics, molasses
- nouns that state a given time, weight, or amount of money
- titles of books, newspapers, television shows, even of plural form

Here are some examples.

- The news was watched by millions.
- Athletics is an important escape for many men.
- Twenty dollars goes fast.
- Forty-five minutes was all the time he could spare.

- *The Times* is known for excellence.
- *Lake Wobegon Days* has won great popularity.

2. Some nouns are commonly plural in usage, even though naming something singular.

- His *trousers* were old and torn.
- The *suds* are almost down the drain.
- *Scissors* are a great invention.
- The *contents* were ruined.

Others include *tweezers, clothes, wages,* and *oats.*

3. Collective nouns can be singular or plural. The decision depends on the speaker's intention. Most modern writers of American English stay with the singular, although usage in the Queen's English differs, with the plural more common in England.

The collective nouns include *family, public, audience, company, flock, team, bunch,* and *committee.*

- The team is practicing.
- The team are discussing last week's game.
- When is the committee meeting?
- The committee are reporting on their various projects.

Note: Many writers simply phrase sentences in another way to avoid the plural verb.

Added Words Affect Agreement

Compound Subjects

Compound subjects joined by *and* are almost always plural.

- Jed and Joyce were arguing animatedly.
- Cashews, olives, and avocados are high in calories.
- Danny and I have never met.

The rare exceptions to this rule are based on the subject's being taken as a single unit.

- Hide and seek is a game I loved as a child.
- My former roommate and still close friend is Laura Radcliff.

There are three possibilities for compound subjects using *or.*

1. Singular words take a singular verb.

- Steak or prime rib is today's choice of entree.

2. Plurals take plural.

- Are the Browns or the Bengals ahead in the game?

3. If subjects differ, the verb agrees with the closer word.

- Jan or her roommates are likely to be home by now.
- Is Jane or her roommates home?

Some Subjects Look Plural But Aren't

- Jan, together with her roommates, is giving a surprise party for Ken.
  (S-V-C) Jan/is giving/party
      How? together with her roommates

Together with, as well as, in addition to, and the like are not conjunctions and therefore do not form compound subjects.
  Watch for such phrases that are not really part of the subject.

- Alice as well as Lydia is interested in trying out for the role.
- The cost of repairs in addition to the purchase price puts the property beyond our reach.

Plus is not a conjunction either.

- A cheeseburger plus fries and a milkshake is loaded with calories.

A Verb Agrees with Its Subject, Not Its Predicate Nominative

- Avocados are the main ingredient in guacamole.

BUT

- The main ingredient in guacamole is avocados.

Identifying the True Subject

- Where are the thumbtacks?
  (S-V) (the) thumbtacks/are
- Which of the twins is taller?
  (S-V-C) which/is/taller
- Which model are you ordering?
  (S-V-O) you/are ordering/model

- There is someone tapping at the door.
    (S-V) someone/is tapping
- There are many unanswered questions.
    (S-V) questions/are

Note: *There*, whether expletive or adverb, does not control the verb. *It*, whether expletive or pronoun, always takes a singular verb.

- It is sunny again today.
- It is my favorite show on television.
- It was a real surprise.

Who or what is the sentence about?
Who or what is doing something?

Those simple questions begin any analysis of how grammar works. They are also the key to solving tricky problems of agreement that depend on knowing which words actually power a sentence, no matter how complicated.

Chapter 23

Forming Comparisons Correctly: A Matter of Degree

good	better	best
bad	worse	worst
many, much	more	most

As with other parts of speech, several of our hardest-working adjectives are irregular in the forms they use to make comparisons. In fact, in order to speak "careful" grammar, it's important to be aware of the exceptions and not to try forcing the exception to fit the rule.

How often do we use comparisons?

- I like this color better than that.
- Jodie's car cost more than mine.
- Steve is the most dependable person I know.

More often than we might guess. They're part of countless advertising claims:

- Maxibrite gets teeth cleaner and whiter!
- You always save more, shopping at ValuePlus!
- It's the store with the MOST!

The question is not only "Are their claims true?" but also "Are the comparisons stated in 'good' grammar?"

Recall that *adjectives can limit*, as in

- This is *my* book.

- I know *that* woman.
- We heard *the* news.

Adjectives can also describe:

- That is a <u>good</u> book.
- I know that <u>young</u> woman.
- We heard the <u>surprising</u> news.

Only descriptive adjectives have comparative forms.

THE THREE DEGREES OF COMPARISON

Positive: Today was <u>warm</u>,
Comparative: but yesterday was <u>warmer</u>.
Superlative: It was the <u>warmest</u> July 5 on record.

1. For most adjectives of one syllable and some of two syllables:
   Comparative—Add an *-er* ending to the positive form.
   Superlative—Add an *-est* ending.

small	smaller	smallest
great	greater	greatest
calm	calmer	calmest

   Note: Some adjectives undergo common spelling changes, such as *y* to *i* before the comparative endings. Remember, the dictionary lists such exceptions.

big	bigger	biggest
fat	fatter	fattest
lovely	lovelier	loveliest
pretty	prettier	prettiest

2. For adjectives of more than two syllables and others hard to pronounce with an *-er* or *-est* ending:

   Comparative—Use the adverb <u>more</u> before the positive form.
   Superlative—Use the adverb <u>most</u> as its indicator.

important	more important	most important
curious	more curious	most curious
sensible	more sensible	most sensible
truthful	more truthful	most truthful

3. Some adjectives of two syllables work either way, depending upon the emphasis desired.

handsome	handsomer	handsomest
	more handsome	most handsome
noble	nobler	noblest
	more noble	most noble
quiet	quieter	quietest
	more quiet	most quiet

4. A number of common adjectives are irregular:

good, well	better	best
little	less, lesser	least
late	later, latter	latest
many, much	more	most
bad, ill	worse	worst
old	older, elder	oldest, eldest
far	farther, further	farthest, furthest
northern	more northern	northernmost*
		*(As with other directions)

TIPS FOR "PERFECT" USAGE

Some adjectives don't lend themselves to comparison. These include *complete*, *perfect*, *universal*, *unanimous*, and *faultless*.

- The crossword puzzle was complete and perfect.
  How could you add anything more?

A word about *unique*—to many purists, *unique* has just one meaning: one of a kind.

- (ouch!) That is a most unique piece of jewelry.
  How can anything be *most* one of a kind?

Unique becomes a weaker, not a stronger word—simply meaning "unusual"—when you try to compare it.

In comparisons, adverbs follow the pattern of adjectives. The comparative and superlative are formed the same way.

fast	faster	fastest
early	earlier	earliest
easily	more easily	most easily
carefully	more carefully	most carefully

HOW THE COMPARATIVE AND SUPERLATIVE DEGREES WORK

Use the comparative for comparing one thing to another.

- Joel is taller than his twin brother.
- I like butterscotch topping better than caramel.
- Jesse drives more carefully than Les.
- Which is the shorter of the two routes?

In using the comparative, make the comparison complete and clear.

- An adult blue whale is larger than any mammal.
  Isn't a blue whale a mammal? If so, add *any other*.
- (clear) An adult blue whale is larger than any other mammal.

- Bea thinks she's smarter than anyone.
  Including herself? If not, add *else*.
- (clear) Bea thinks she's smarter than anyone else.

- Maxibrite gets teeth cleaner and whiter!
  Than shoe polish? Shampoo? Deodorant?
- (clear) Maxibrite gets teeth cleaner and whiter than any other toothpaste.

Oh, you know what I meant! Even so, it's best to assume that words and sentences *do* mean what they say. Otherwise, there would be nothing to do but guess. One of the best reasons for following rules of grammar is that they give a starting point for reaching an understanding of one another's words and ideas. Often it doesn't matter, but faulty phrasing can sometimes lead to serious misunderstandings.

Here are more ways comparisons can cause confusion.

- A vacation in Mexico is less expensive than Europe.
  Comparing *vacation* to *Europe*?
- (better) A vacation in Mexico is less expensive than one in Europe.

- (confusing) I respect Bob more than Andy.
  Which way should this be taken?
- (clear) I have more respect for Bob than for Andy.
          or
       I respect Bob more than Andy does.

Use the superlative only for comparing more than two things.

- Kip is the most optimistic person I know.
- My most comfortable pair of jeans is also my oldest pair.
- Shakespeare's *Hamlet* is considered the greatest tragedy ever written in English.

Note: With superlative comparisons, use *all*, not *any*.

- Marty thinks roses are the prettiest of any flower.
- (correct) Marty thinks roses are the prettiest flower of all.

PRACTICE

In the following sentences, identify the confusing or incorrect use of words in making comparisons.

1. Aunt Addie's angel food cake is always most perfect.
2. I like the Corvette better than any car.
3. Which city is biggest, San Diego or San Francisco?
4. I can't understand Meredith as well as Hildy.
5. This problem is the most difficult of any.
6. Dee comes to work earlier than anyone on the staff.
7. There is now more universal agreement on the need to control pollution of the atmosphere.
8. Coming to work by bus is more economical than taxi.
9. What is the northernest state in the United States?
10. My home is nearer to Lake Huron than any Great Lake.

(For answers, see page 201.)

Chapter 24

How to Make Yourself More Effective in English

SEVEN KEY STEPS TO BETTER USAGE

1. *Don't let sloppy, everyday speech become an unbreakable habit.*

   "I'm gunna go" instead of "I'm going to go."
   "I wanna," "I gotta,"—Americans are always in a hurry, and even our speech shows it.

   As native speakers of English, we understand each other, but this leads to illiteracies such as:

   "cuz" for *because*
   "woulda" or "would of" for *would have*
   "wanna" for *want to*

2. *Be careful in your use of personal pronouns.* Make a special point to watch out for compound subjects and objects. No one is so illiterate as to say, "Me is Joe Bumpkin." But something happens when a sentence should begin, "Mel and I are...." Perhaps *and* gets confused with a preposition. Yet that doesn't explain why no one will mistakenly say, "Wait for I," but will use the wrong pronoun when it should be, "Wait for Mel and me."
   Check to see how a pronoun works and watch for compound usage. Then picking the correct pronoun should be a matter of course.

3. *Make the right choice between the past and the past participle of irregular verbs.* Being effective in grammar does not mean knowing the difference between a gerund and participle. It means making the right choices when you speak and write. It means saying

   "I sang," not "I sung"
   "I brought," not "I brung"

"I have gone," not "I have went"
"I saw," not "I seen"

Understanding grammar helps you see the reason for the correct choice, but making the choice is also a matter of practice.

4. *Pay particular attention to* doesn't *and* don't. Remember,

It doesn't.
She doesn't.
He doesn't.
This pen doesn't work.
Tracy doesn't work.

Incorrect use of this one little word, for many a troublesome choice in the third person singular, is almost enough to label you illiterate all by itself.

"Doesn't" sounds similar to *hasn't* and *isn't* in its contracted form with *not*. All are used in the same way. Try to remember words that are formed alike, sound similar, and work alike. When you've seen a pattern, the right choice comes more easily.

5. *Don't try to qualify adjectives with unrelated words that have no real business there.* Break the habit of putting such words as *sorta, kinda, real,* and *pretty* in such sentences as "It was a good game," "So-and-so seems nice," and "I'm tired."

Versions of these "uncultivated" expressions have parts to play in sentences, but they shouldn't be asked to do the word of an adverb.

What's the best way to correct the error? Just leave them out entirely. Saying "I sorta like you" is not just "bad" grammar. It leaves the impression that the person saying it lacks the confidence to express his opinion directly. It is correct to say

- I enjoy that kind of music.
- This is not my sort of exercise.

And, of course, if you think someone or something is pretty, say so.

6. *Make sure that the verb agrees with its subject.*

7. *Watch your spelling.* In writing, it may be the first impression you make. Poor spelling can make a lastingly bad one.

What has spelling got to do with grammar? To many, it shows a confusion about the rules of grammar to mix up such words as:

you're	your	
they're	their	there
it's	its	

It helps to remember that they all belong to sets of look-alike words that also work in the same way.

There and *here* are adverbs that answer *where?*

You're, *they're*, and *it's* are subject + verb in a contraction, with an apostrophe as their special sign.

Your, *its*, and *their*, along with *her*, *his*, and *our*, are the set of possessives, all look-alikes as well.

Another troublesome trio is *two*, *to*, and *too*.

two = the number 2
  to = the preposition and sign of an infinitive

The real troublemaker is *too*. More often than not, *too* does *not* have the same meaning as also. Look at the extra o, and think of *too* as a little word that stretches out the quality an adjective or adverb expresses.

- Maggie is t-o-o-o-o thin.
- That ring is t-o-o-o expensive.
- You are t-o-o eager.
- This is too much.

How we speak depends on many things. It may vary with the occasion, just as we dress formally sometimes and casually others. Yet it's important to be aware of the choices being made and the reasons behind those choices. That awareness is the key to putting grammar effectively to work.

Chapter 25

The Complete Sentence: Putting It All Together

What is a good sentence?
One that works.

By its classic definition, a sentence is a group of words that expresses a complete thought. True. Our system of grammar also shows that an English sentence is powered by a subject and a verb, in that order.

Then what about the three-word answer at the beginning of this chapter? Is it a sentence or just a piece or fragment of a sentence? Which is more effective as an answer to the question, "What is a good sentence?"

- One that works.
- A good sentence is one that works.

The second "correct" version, which fits the textbook definition, dilutes the surprise. The first, by example, makes the point that the textbook definition isn't literally true. It delivers its message in the fewest words possible and gives its hearer something to think about. What more could you ask of a sentence?

ELLIPSES

Many sentences omit words that are automatically understood and don't need to be repeated.

- A sentence expresses a complete thought.
  (S-V-C) sentence/expresses/(a) thought

- True.
    (S-V-C) That/is/true

There are **elliptical** sentences, clauses, and phrases. Ellipses are perfectly correct when they leave no doubt about what is omitted. In fact, we object to sentences that repeat what we have every reason to know.

Ellipsis accounts for the fact that some words in sentences don't seem to work in the regular way. The words that complete the thought are not directly stated but understood.

For example, ellipsis takes place with every use of a compound subject and verb, and also with imperatives.

- Pepe and Abbie just arrived.
    Pepe [just arrived] and Abbie just arrived.
- Hyland opened the door and walked in.
    Hyland opened the door and [Hyland] walked in.
- Come here.
    [You] come here.

Because ours is a language of word order, the fluent speaker "hears" and automatically understands what is missing.

Unfortunately, some students of grammar try to force every sentence to fit the definition rather than the way grammar actually works. They write stiff and awkward sentences that may be "right" according to the rules, but are not actually good.

Here are some more examples of ellipsis at work

a. He trusts her and she him.
b. I will take the chance if you will, too.
c. While in Mexico, Whit studied Spanish.
d. My brother Vince is younger than I.

We don't "feel" anything missing, and it's easy to supply the understood words.

a. He trusts her and she [trusts] him.
b. I will take the chance if you will [take the chance], too.
c. While [he was] in Mexico, Whit studied Spanish.
d. My brother Vince is younger than I [am young].

Of course, if there is doubt, words must be included.

- I understand Glen better than you.
    Better than I do you?
    Better than you do?

The revised versions may still be elliptical.

- I understand Glen better than you do. [understand Glen]
- I understand Glen better than I can [understand] you.

The purpose of a sentence is to deliver a thought, be it a statement, question, exclamation, or command. A good writer does not have grammar on his mind when he sits down to write. He has an idea he needs to express. It's silly to imagine F. Scott Fitzgerald saying, "Now, I think I'll write a compound-complex sentence with an introductory adverb clause and a couple of infinitive phrases." He had something more important on his mind, *The Great Gatsby*.

In spite of what some guides seem to imply, an understanding of grammar is more important in reading and correcting errors than in helping a person write good sentences.

KEEP IT SIMPLE

A sentence should be no more complex than the thought it has to convey.

A complex thought can require a complex sentence.
A simple sentence fits a simple and direct idea best.

Sometimes people feel that "dressing up" a sentence improves it, as this anecdote shows. It is told by Richard P. Feynman in his book, *Surely You're Joking, Mr. Feynman!*

There was a sociologist who had written a paper for us all to read—something he had written ahead of time. I started to read the damn thing, and my eyes were coming out: I couldn't make head or tail of it! I figured it was because I hadn't read any of the books on that list. I had this uneasy feeling of "I'm not adequate," until finally I said to myself, "I'm gonna stop, and read one *sentence* slowly, *so I can figure out what the hell it means."*

So I stopped—at random—and read the next sentence very carefully. I can't remember it precisely, but it was very close to this: "The individ-

ual member of the social community often receives his information via visual, symbolic channels." I went back and forth over it, and translated. You know what it means? "People read."

Then I went over the next sentence, and I realized that I could translate that one also. Then it became a kind of empty business: "Sometimes people read; sometimes people listen to the radio," and so on, but written in such a fancy way that I couldn't understand it at first, and when I finally deciphered it, there was nothing in it.

Sometimes complex sentences and difficult words are nothing more than a way to impress others and make ordinary thoughts sound beyond the reach of someone who does not think of himself as an expert.

Also notice how Feynman, a Nobel prize winner and one of the world's greatest theoretical physicists, carefully and purposely avoids seeming stuffy by using expressions such as "I'm gonna stop" and "what the hell" when he writes.

WHAT IS A SENTENCE FRAGMENT?

One that works.

Would anyone really write that as a sentence, all by itself? It doesn't make sense in answer to the question, "What is a fragment?" Yet it made perfect sense before.

According to the grammar book definition, a **fragment** is a group of words that doesn't express a complete thought and cannot stand alone as a sentence. Most so-called fragments are really punctuation errors. A writer sometimes uses a period by mistake, thereby separating a phrase or a clause from the rest of its sentence. It may not be clear whether this separated piece or fragment belongs to the sentence before or after it.

Example

- I was totally taken by surprise. When Eric called last night on the phone. I didn't even recognize his voice at first.

"When Eric . . . phone" is often called a fragment. It can be correctly punctuated two ways.

- I was totally taken by surprise when Eric called last night on the phone. I didn't even recognize his voice at first.
- I was totally taken by surprise. When Eric called last night on the phone, I didn't even recognize his voice at first.

Run-on sentences are also caused by mistakes in punctuation.

- Only the other day I was thinking how long it has been since I heard from him, you can imagine how glad I was that he called.

The mistake is the comma between *him* and *you*, which is not strong enough to join the two parts. *Among the ways to correct it*:

> . . . him. You . . .
>
> . . . him; you . . .
>
> . . . him, so you . . .

QUALITIES THAT COUNT IN WRITING GOOD SENTENCES

1. Keep to the natural order unless there's an important reason for changing it.

- The rabbit came out of the magician's hat.
- Out of the magician's hat came the rabbit.

Transposing won't make a mundane idea seem inspired.

2. Use the passive voice only when the subject or actor is unimportant.

- Chains kept the prisoner from reaching the window.
- The prisoner was kept from reaching the window by the chains.

Sentences move faster in the active voice.

3. Make sure that there is a clear reference for every pronoun.

- Ron told his boss that he didn't understand him.

Who doesn't understand whom? Sometimes it *does* get tricky.

- Ron accused the boss of misunderstanding him.
- Ron, not understanding his boss, asked him what he meant.

4. Don't allow too many words to get between a subject and its verb.

- Early the next morning, the first thing Marcie did after turning off the alarm clock and putting on a robe and slippers was to go out on the balcony and look once again at the lovely view of the mountains.

$$(\text{S-V}) \; \text{thing/was/} \begin{cases} \text{to go} \\ \text{(and)} \\ \text{(to) look} \end{cases}$$

- (better) Early the next morning, after turning off the alarm clock and putting on her robe and slippers, Marcie went out on the balcony and looked once again at the lovely view of the mountains.

$$(S-V)\ Marcie/\begin{cases} went \\ (and) \\ looked \end{cases}$$

5. Avoid repeating a word unless your purpose is to call attention to it.

- His face told me the news before he spoke. I could hardly face it. I turned my face to hide the sudden rush of emotion before turning to face him again.

A reader will get stuck in all the *faces* and hardly be able to make sense of the whole.

6. Be careful not to create confusion by putting words close together in a sentence if they have similar forms but different uses.

- Chet wanted to fish and to loaf, and to Tammy that was a boring kind of vacation.

The reader expects another infinitive instead of the prepositional phrase, *to Tammy*.

- While I was waiting, watching the others sitting in the waiting room amused me greatly.

In a verb phrase, then as a gerund, and finally as a participial adjective, the *-ing*s in this sentence become confusing.

- (better) Chet wanted to fish and to loaf, but Tammy thought that kind of vacation was boring.
- (better) While I waited, I amused myself greatly by watching the others with me in the waiting room.

7. Assume you will be taken literally. Don't leave out necessary words that will make your meaning clear.

- I have no need nor interest in your help.
- (better) I have no need *for* nor interest in your help.
- Checking the balance, a $200 error was found.
- (clear) Checking the balance, I found a $200 error.

8. Make sure that a sentence really says what you mean it to say. Writing speaks for you, but it also must speak for itself. Try to leave no gaps, loopholes, or questions that the sentence itself doesn't answer.

As a final step in writing, read your words as if you were a stranger to them. This is the time when your understanding of grammar is helpful, when you check to be sure you've expressed yourself clearly.

SAMPLES OF TODAY'S GOOD WRITING

Consider the following examples from three respected magazines. Be aware of the subject/verb/complement in each sentence. Notice how modifying phrases and clauses expand on the basic Actor/Action core, and observe the techniques each writer uses to subordinate these ideas to the main thought. The first passage is from Edna O'Brien's "Sleepwalking at the Ritz."

> *I decided to take a boat trip to see the whales. This was not to be a replay of Captain Ahab's metaphysical quest; it was thirty or forty fairly sedate people boarding near the restaurant Proud Mary's, then standing on the deck while the skipper, whom we could not see, talked over the loudspeaker, expressing the wish that we would have "real fun" and that the whales "would show up okay." There we were, cruising along at ten knots—he told us that he did not want to spook the whales—when all of a sudden his voice rose an octave: He had sighted one. As it rose and rippled like a great gray tankard, the cameras clicked and the boat came almost to a standstill. Like most excitements it was brief, and the rest of the journey was ocean and sky, which in the haze appeared as one.*

Notice how O'Brien puts quotation marks around the Captain's words. The fact that they are not in "choice" English gives a more vivid impression of the Captain and adds a personal touch to the description. Notice also how O'Brien uses punctuation as a guide to the desired reading of her sentences.

Each writer has a style, a way of writing, that is as individual as a speaking voice. A person can also use a variety of styles to suit different occasions—formal or informal, journalistic or chatty.

Compare the paragraph by O'Brien with the following one from "Dime-Store Doughboys" by Henry Kurtz. How are their writing styles different? Which makes greater use of phrases and subordinate clauses? Which makes greater use of factual adjectives? In dealing with complex styles, check for the S-V-C of subordinate clauses, too, and notice the questions being answered by different elements of the sentence.

> *Commercially made metal toy soldiers date back to the late eighteenth century, when German tinsmiths began casting two-dimensional or "flat" figures of the sort immortalized by Hans Christian Andersen in "The Steadfast Tin Soldier." European firms went on to develop sturdier, solid-cast three-dimensional figures of lead alloy, and in the 1890s an English toy maker named William Britain revolutionized the field with a line of less costly hollow-cast toy troops. However, it wasn't until the 1930s that the United States developed a uniquely American toy soldier. Sold mainly in the five-and-dime stores, especially the F. W. Woolworth chain, they came to be know as dime-store soldiers.*

Now read the following paragraph from John Berger's "The Credible Word."

> *One does not look through writing onto reality—as through a clean or dirty windowpane. Words are never transparent. They create their own space, the space of experience, not that of existence. Clarity of the written word has little to do with style. A baroque text can be clear; a simple one can be dim. Clarity, in my view, is a gift of the way the space created by words in a given text is arranged.*
>
> *The task of arranging this space is not unlike that of furnishing and arranging a home. The aim is similar: to accommodate with ease what belongs there and to welcome those who enter. . . .*

(S-V-C) Clarity/is/(a) gift

Berger does not speak of grammar, he speaks of space and compares writing to decorating a home.

(S-V-C) (The) aim/is/similar
How? to accommodate with ease
(and)
to welcome

Berger writes of space being "arranged." Although he does not mention grammar, it is the system of English word order that provides both the freedom and the space. Within it are endless possibilities of "furnishing" with words yet maintaining the "gift" of clarity.

From every well-written sentence, no matter how complicated, radiates the underlying force of the subject/verb/complement which powers it all.

(S-V-C) (the) force/radiates

Once you can recognize this force at work, you have discovered the key to how English grammar works and can go on to develop an increased understanding and greater appreciation of how "the space created by words . . . is arranged."

Appendix

Answers

Pages 10–11. Nouns

1. naturalist; 2. moments; 3. thrill; 4. beauty; 5. complexity; 6. life; 7. feeling; 8. depression; 9. lifetime; 10. span; 11. paradise; 12. wonders; 13. world; 14. feeling; 15. time; 16. beauty; 17. variety; 18. lushness; 19. forest; 20. maze; 21. trees; 22. gardens; 23. orchids; 24. web; 25. creepers; 26. species; 27. number; 28. forms; 29. time; 30. congregation; 31. mammals; 32. conglomeration; 33. birds; 34. butterfly; 35. dragonfly; 36. cocoon; 37. stick; 38. leaf; 39. insect; 40. piece; 41. shade; 42. herd; 43. zebras; 44. school; 45. dolphins; 46. eye; 47. world; 48. spider; 49. body; 50. line; 51. transport; 52. exploration; 53. world

Page 13. Using The *as a Determiner*

It is possible to use the following as nouns in sentences: 1, 2, 3, 5, 7, 8, 9, 11, 13, 14, 16, 20, 22, 23, 25, 26, 27, 28, 30. Some can work more than one way, depending on the sentence.

Page 16. Practice in Finding the Subject

1. (The) clown; 2. (The) leader; 3. (A) friend; 4. Yolanda; 5. (The) weather; 6. (the) judge; 7. Crenshaw

Page 20. Practice with Subjects and Verbs

1. passengers/crammed; 2. members/disagreed; 3. candidate/promised; 4. noise/startled; 5. experts/predicted; 6. player/hurtled; 7. Jensen/leaped

Pages 25–26. Practice Using Irregular Verbs

1. frozen; 2. begin; 3. chose; 4. blown; 5. threw; 6. gives; 7. seen; 8. drank; 9. fallen; 10. come, came, come

Page 36. Matching Up Pronouns

1. he/Jon; 2. he/unclear; 3. they/jokes, he/Luke; 4. it/blizzard; it/cabin; they/people

Page 37. Pronouns in Action

1–3. I, me, I—person speaking; 4. he—teacher; 5. him—General; 6. them—people. 7. He—General; 8. We—person speaking + priest; 9. it—door; 10. He—young man; 11. It—flat; 12–18. he—professor

Page 42. Adjectives in Action

1. flying; 2. Another; 3. large; 4. round; 5. inert; 6. invisible; 7. Georges'; 8. fixed; 9. fishing; 10. whole; 11. hulking; 12. great; 13. Georges'; 14. severed; 15. wave; 16. record; 17. disappointed; 18. moderate; 19. day's; 20. noon; 21. lateral; 22. twenty-four; 23. starboard; 24. Ra's; 25. lower; 26. steering; 27. ankle-deep; 28. life; 29. every; 30. holding

Note: *Adjective* is a term used to name the way a word works. Some grammarians called words like *Georges'* and *Ra's* possessive nouns, although they work like adjectives. It is also correct to list *the*, the determiner of a noun, as an adjective, as well as *our* and *containing*.

Page 48. Adverbs in Action

1. frantically; 2. up; 3. up; 4. there; 5. in; 6. hastily; 7. frantically; 8. directly; 9. up

Page 53. Prepositional Phrases Used as Adjectives

1. in the movie—scene, near the beginning—one, with loads—one, of laughs—loads; 2. of the alarm clock—call, about a life—dream, of leisure—life, in Tahiti—life; 3. of geese—gaggle, for a group—term, of these fowl creatures—group; 4. upon the post—sign, about the dangerous condition—warning, of the old bridge—condition; 5. of light—gleam, through the farmhouse windows—light, of the tired man—hope

Page 53. Prepositional Phrases as Adverbs

1. until this year—worked, for a Tucson newspaper—worked; 2. after the game—rushed, out of the stadium—rushed, toward their cars—rushed; 3. in the plane's belly—can put, under their seats—can put, in overhead compartments—can put; 4. at heart—young, because of their optimistic attitudes—succeed; 5. by hand—was written, in an almost illegible scrawl—was written

Pages 55–56. Prepositions and Adverbs in Action

Prepositional Phrases: 1. from the fire—roar; 2. into camp—rained; 3. across the ground—swirled; 4. in the churning air—swirled; 5. by midafternoon—reached; 6. by the heavy desert winds—driven; 7. of East Dune—top; 8. for a moment—paused; 9. at the tall grasses and lower branches—licking; 10. of a tree—branches; 11. to the top—leaped; 12. into a thirty-foot torch—turning; 12. of fire—line; 13. like flares—exploded; 14. to the flames—fed; 15. down the duneslopes—spurred; 16. toward the riverbed—spurred; 17. at an incredible speed—spurred; 18. through grass and bush—sweeping; 19. for that sight—could have prepared; 20. across the dune tops—marched; 21. into the Kalahari—marched; 22. like a spectacular sunset—lighting; 23. behind it—remained; 24. of burned-out trees and logs—glow; 25. in the blush—lost; 26. of dawn—blush.
Adverbs: 1. on; 2. harder; 3. quickly; 4. on.

Page 64. Working with Conjunctions

Simple Sentences: 1. The strong wind and driving rain; 2. mislaid his billfold but found it in his car; 3. both Beth and her parents; 4. neither hear nor see; 5. the moon and the stars, glowed and gleamed
Compound Sentences: 1.d; 2.f; 3.b; 4.h; 5.e; 6.a; 7.g; 8.c

Page 74. Working with Four Types of Sentences

1. statement; 2. question; 3. command; 4. statement; 5. exclamation; 6. exclamation; 7. question; 8. command

Page 77. Practice Turning Statements into Questions

1. Has Chris forgotten his promise? 2. Can you understand his point of view? 3. When will Bonnie be home? *or* Will Bonnie be home tomorrow? 4. How much did the car repairs cost? 5. Which car did Sarah choose? 6. Was the magician clever?

Page 95. Working with Be

1. scorer, pred. noun; 2. good, pred. adj.; 3. no complement; 4. difficult, pred. adj.; 5. no complement; 6. choice, pred. noun; 7. careful, pred. adj.

Page 97. Working with the Progressive Form of Verbs

1. We/are counting—intransitive; 2. Nora (and) Ted/have been saving/money (direct object) transitive; 3. baby/was being/angel (pred. noun)—linking; 4. company/will be using/system (direct object)—transitive; 5. You/are promising/deal (direct object)—transitive; 6. chipmunk/had been nibbling/blossoms (direct object)—transitive; 7. we/will have been waiting—intransitive; 8. children/were being/quiet (pred. adj.)—linking

Page 99. Working with Active and Passive Voice

1. (S-V-C) (The) lawyer/question/Sylvia—Active (Sylvia was questioned by the lawyer about her whereabouts on the night of May 17.); 2. (S-V) Many/were (not) televised—Passive (The networks did not televise many of the regular shows Monday because of the playoffs.); 3. (S-V-C) People/will have heard/(the) news—Active (The news will have been heard by people around the world at almost the same instant.); 4. (S-V) Pictures/are shown—Passive (Harry shows the latest pictures of his grandson to everyone.); 5. (S-V) (The) Oscar/will be given—Passive (The Motion Picture Academy will give the Oscar for best picture last.); 6. (S-V) Most/was eaten—Passive (My little brother ate most of the chocolate cake.); 7. (S-V-C) I/have spoken/word—Active (My last word on the subject has been spoken.)

Page 105. When Personal Pronouns Become a Problem

1. you/me—objects of preposition; we—subject; project—direct object; success—objective complement; 2. Bob/I—subjects; salad—direct object; ants—object of preposition; 3. Mr. Walsh—object of preposition; guarantee—subject;

job—object of preposition; wife/him—retained indirect objects; mechanic—object of preposition; 4. sports/affairs—objects of preposition; people—subject; us/them—objects of preposition; 5. Gloria—noun of direct address; you/he—subjects; you—subject; me—direct object; procrastinator—objective complement

Pages 105–106. Compound Confusion Causes Mistakes with Pronouns

1. her; 2. them; 3. her, me; 4. he, I; 5. he

Pages 111–112. Participles at Work

1. typed in red—manuscript; 2. smiling—face, wounded—pride; 3. driven by the wind—clouds, changing—weather; 4. coded—message, missing—treasure; 5. knowing the truth—anyone, boasting—claims; 6. wearing that color—you; 7. stolen in the robbery—money

Pages 114–115. Gerunds and Participles in Action

1. are having—verb phrase; 2. keeping it—gerund (subject); 3. have been thinking—verb phrase, selling the rattling old collection of scrap metal—gerund phrase (obj. of prep.), rattling—adjective; 4. broken down—participial phrase, driving—gerund (obj. of prep.); 5. joking—adjective, retiring it—gerund (obj. of prep.); 6. Judging by its resale value—participial phrase, being junked—gerund (dir. obj.); 7. Loved by no one, wanted by no one—participial phrases, is facing—verb phrase, failing—adjective

Page 118. Working with Infinitive Phrases

1. to make the short yardage—direct object; 2. to be there on time—adverb; 3. to please someone difficult to please—adjective, (difficult) to please—adverb; 4. To like oneself—subject; 5. to be their role models—adjective; 6. to hear the judges' decision—adverb; 7. to travel in space—predicate noun

Page 124. Practice in Punctuating Quotations

1. Wade said, "I hope you understand my point of view."
2. "Please give me one more chance," Bert begged.
3. Dan declared, "I need more time to think."
4. "What are you doing?" asked Alice.
5. "I am on my hands and knees," explained Ed, "to look for my lost contact lenses."
6. "His actions confused me, too," replied Ruth.
7. "Just listen to my side of the story," Paul pleaded.
8. Ted told Terry, "You have the wrong idea."
9. "Look out!" cried Cathy. "You're going to run into that door!"
10. "Someone watching," observed Otis, "wouldn't understand this at all."

Page 131. Adverb Clauses in Action

Main Clause (S-V-C)	Dependent Clause (S-V-C)
1. We/have heard	he/left
	Sub. Conj.—since
2. You/have/magazines	you/are waiting
	Sub. Conj.—while
3. Fred/plays/tennis	he/gets/plenty
	Sub. Conj.—as if
4. system/saves/time	it/combines/steps
	Sub. Conj.—because
5. you/find/object	you/put/it
	Sub. Conj.—where

Page 132. More Practice with Adverb Clauses

1. (S-V) Sandy/picked
   How? as if she didn't really like it
       (S-V-C) she/did(n't) like/it
2. (S-V-C) You/can(n't) be/sure
   When? until you have tried it
       (S-V-C) you/have tried/it
3. (S-V-C) I/will try/(a) bite.
   Why? Since squid sounds unappetizing to me
       (S-V-C) squid/sounds/unappetizing
4. (S-V-C) Carol/can find/little
   When? when she eats at fast food restaurants
       (S-V) she/eats
5. (S-V-C) you/will enjoy/(a) piece
   When? After you finish
       (S-V) you/finish
   How? if you have any appetite left
       (S-V-C) you/have/appetite
6. (S-V-C) I/will meet/you
   Where? wherever you say
       (S-V) you/say
   When? Whenever the time is convenient for you
       (S-V-C) (the) time/is/convenient
7. (S-V) We/will be working
   Why? because many details need testing
       (S-V-C) details/need/testing
   When? before the prototype is okayed
       (S-V) (the) prototype/is okayed

Page 137. Working with Adjective Clauses

1. that has a good beat—music (essential); 2. whom I asked—people (essential), which recently went into effect—ruling (nonessential); 3. which she named

Beeper—kitten (nonessential); 4. when you locked yourself out of your apartment—time (essential); 5. that I just finished—novel (essential), who prefers a happy ending—anyone (essential)

Page 137. Combining Sentences

1. The director, who is a perfectionist, called extra rehearsals.
2. The joke has a punch line that I don't understand.
3. Mr. Carlson, who is considered an authority on the Civil War, is a retired army officer.
4. Everyone had trusted the company president, who was accused of embezzlement.
5. Kent, who rarely loses his temper, is a natural leader.
   Kent is a natural leader who rarely loses his temper.

Pages 138–139. Identifying Adjective and Adverb Clauses

1. When we came into the ski lodge—adverb (*when?*); 2. which seemed high enough to me—adjective (slope); 3. Before we left for the ski resort—adverb (*when?*), that looked perfect for a pro—adjective (outfit); 4. before I started downhill—adjective (moment), when I wished to be somewhere else—adjective (time); 5. Although I tried not to show it—adverb (negative *how?*), who was full of panic—adjective (someone); 6. When I reached the bottom of the slope—adverb (*when?*), which had seemed so steep—adjective (slope); 7. where I had first tried skiing—adjective (slope), even though my friends call it a molehill—adverb (negative *why?*)

Page 139. What Words Do

1. before—preposition;   2. before—adverb;   3. before—relative adverb; 4. before—subordinating conjunction;   5. After—preposition;   6. After—subordinating conjunction; 7. after—adjective

Page 143. Identifying Noun Clauses

1. why Hubie felt embarrassed—direct object; 2. whoever calls—subject; 3. what is best for them—direct object; 4. whatever flavor you like—predicate nominative; 5. what you told me—object of preposition; 6. whomever you call—indirect object, how important the meeting is—direct object; 7. where he has gone—subject

Pages 154–155. Working with the Subjunctive Mood

1. were; 2. be; 3. were; 4. stay; 5. were; 6. address; 7. were.

Page 156. The Transitive Trio

1. We/have set/hopes; 2. (The) fans/raised/voices (and) sang/(the) song; 3. (The) referee/laid/(the) ball; 4. (The) quarterback/will set/record; 5. spirits/were raised; 6. (The) coach/is laying/groundwork; 7. we/will raise/(the) banner

Pages 156–157. The Intransitive Trio

1. (a) fog/lay; 2. (the) sun/had risen, blobs/were sitting; 3. (A) dog/was lying; 4. (The) farmer/rose; 5. (An) trunk/had lain; 6. boys/sat, another/lay; 7. (The) level/was rising

Page 157. All Six Together

1. risen; 2. sat; 3. lain; 4. rising; 5. set; 6. lying; 7. raised; 8. lain; 9. laid; 10. sit.

Page 158. More Common "Problem" Verbs

1. gone; 2. did, did; 3. ran; 4. run; 5. saw; 6. come; 7. came

Page 160. Correcting Errors

1. I didn't mean to insult anybody. 2. It doesn't matter to me. 3. Hank could have gone back to work. 4. I came right after you called. 5. If I were you, I wouldn't tell anybody what I did. 6. The old dog would have lain there all day. 7. There wasn't anybody sitting in the front row. 8. The neighbors did all they could have to help. 9. We never had any doubt that we saw a genius at work. 10. When Monday came, we would have welcomed another weekend.

Page 168. Making Sentence Parts Agree

1. is; 2. has, its; 3. are; 4. Are; 5. is; 6. are; 7. are, is; 8. are, was; 9. is; 10. is, are.

Page 179. Catching Errors in Comparison

1. Aunt Addie's angel food cake is always perfect.
2. I like the Corvette better than any other car.
3. Which city is bigger, San Diego or San Francisco?
4. I can't understand Meredith as well as I can Hildy; or I can't understand Meredith as well as Hildy can.
5. This problem is the most difficult of all.
6. Dee comes to work earlier than anyone else on the staff.
7. There is now more nearly universal agreement on the need to control pollution of the atmosphere.
8. Coming to work by bus is more economical than coming by taxi.
9. What is the northernmost state in the United States?
10. My home is nearer to Lake Huron than to any other Great Lake.

Index

A

Active voice, verb, 97
Adjective(s), 39–42
  comparison of, 175–179
  defined, 39, 67
  noun used as, 41
  participle, 110
  predicate adjective, 93
  prepositional phrase used as, 51–52
  that limit by number, 41–42
Adjective clause, 132–137
  essential or nonessential, 135
  relative adjective in, 136–137
  relative adverb in, 135–136
  relative pronoun in, 133
Adverb(s), 43–48
  comparison of, 176
  defined, 43, 67
  distinguishing from preposition, 55
  infinitive used as, 117
  not, 47
  prepositional phrase used as, 53
  use of, 45
Adverb clause, 130–132
  punctuation of, 131–132
  subordinating conjunctions with, 130
Adverbial noun, 45
Agreement of pronoun and antecedent, 36, 164–167
Agreement of subject and verb, 170–173
Apostrophe, 106–108, 124–125
Appositive, 82, 86, 141
Auxiliary verb (helping verb), 25, 96

B

Be, 91–99
  forms of, 95–99
  uses of, 92–95

C

Capital letters, 13
Case use, nouns/pronouns, 101–105
Clause, 130–137
  adjective, 132–137
  adverb, 130–132
  dependent, 130
  essential, 135
  independent, 129
  nonessential, 135
  noun, 139–143
Collective noun, 171
Colon, 125–127
Combining sentences, 129–143
Comma, 62, 65, 81–83
Command, 73, 75, 80
Comparison, 175–179
Complement, 29–32
  defined, 31
  direct object, 31
  predicate adjective, 93
  predicate nominative, 101, 103–104
  subjective, 31
Complete predicate, 93–94
Complete subject, 93–94
Complex sentence, 129–143
Compound parts, 59–60

Compound sentence, 59–60
  defined, 59, 129
  punctuation, 59, 64–65, 83
Compound subject, 171–172
Compound-complex sentence,
    145
Conjunction, 57–65
  and, 57–60
  coordinating, 62–63
  paired, 63
  subordinating, 130

D

Dangling modifier
  infinitive, 116
  participle, 113
Dashes, 84
Declarative sentence, 73, 74
Determiners, 12–13
Direct object, 30, 101
Doesn't, don't, 182
Double negative, 159–160

E

Ellipsis, 84, 185–187
End marks, 79–80
Exclamation, 74, 75, 80
Exclamation point, 74, 79
Exclamatory sentence, 75
Expletive: *it, there*, 94–95, 117–118,
    173

F

5 W's and an H, 85–90
Fragment, 188–189
Future perfect tense, 22, 23
Future tense, 22–24

G

Grammar, definition, 3
Gerund, 113–114

H

Helping verb, 24
  be as helper, 94

I

Imperative mood, 152
Imperative sentence, 75
Indefinite pronoun, 164–167
Independent clause, 59, 129
Indicative mood, 152
Indirect object, 103
Infinitive, 115–119
  splitting of, 160–161
Interjection, 67, 80
Interrogative sentence, 73–74, 75
Intransitive verb, 30, 94
Irregular verbs, 23–24, 27, 157–158
Italics, 125

K

Kind, sort, type, 46

L

Lie, lay, 155–156
Linking verb, 31, 92–94

M

Mood
  imperative, 152
  indicative, 152
  subjunctive, 152–154

N

Natural or normal word order, 72, 73,
    94
Nominative case, 101
Nonessential clause, 135
Not, 47–48
Noun, 7–13
  abstract, 9

case use, subject, 15–16
concrete, 9
defined, 9, 67
determiner of, 12–13
gerund, 113–114
predicate, 93, 101
proper, 13
used as adjective, 41
Noun of address, 82
Noun clause, 139–143
Number, personal pronoun, 34–36

O

Object of preposition, 49
Object of verb
direct object, 30
indirect object, 103
Objective case, 102, 103–105
Objective complement, 103–104

P

Parentheses, 84
Participial phrase, 110–112
Participles, 109–110
dangling, 113
past participle, 109
present participle, 96, 109
Parts of speech
adjective, 39–42
adverb, 43–48
conjunction, 57–65
determined by use, 10
formal definition, 67
interjection, 67, 80
noun, 7–13
preposition, 49–56
pronoun, 33–37
term defined, 15
verb, 17–27
Passive voice, 97–99, 104, 109
Past participle, 109
Past perfect tense, 22
Past tense, 21, 22, 23, 24
Perfect tenses, 22, 23, 161–162

Period, use of, 79, 80
Personal pronoun, 33–37, 101, 107
Phrase
adjective, 51–53
adverb, 53
appositive, 141
defined, 52
gerund, 113–114
infinitive, 115–118
participial phrase, 110–112
prepositional, 49, 51–53
verb, 95–97
verbal, 109–119
Possessive case, 106–108
use with gerund, 115
Predicate
complete, 58
compound, 59
defined, 58
Predicate adjective, 93
Predicate noun, 93, 101
agreement of, 170–171
Preposition(s), 49–56
commonly used, chart of, 50
defined, 50, 67
distinguished from adverbs, 54–55
of more than one word, 51
Prepositional phrase, 49, 51–53
adjective phrase, 51–52
adverb phrase, 53
defined, 49
object of, defined, 49
Present participle, 96, 109
Present perfect tense, 22
Present tense, 22
Principal parts of verbs, 21–22, 24
background, 21
irregular verbs, 23–24
regular verbs, 21–22
Progressive forms, 95–97, 109
Pronoun, 33–37
agreement, 36, 164–167
case forms, 101–105, 107
compound personal, 168–170
defined, 33, 67
demonstrative, 167–168

Pronoun (*continued*)
  indefinite, 164–167
  number, 34–35
  objective case, 102, 103–105
  personal, 34–36
  possessive, 134
  reflexive, 169
  relative, 133
  replacing subject, 35, 36, 102
  special problems, 36, 102
Proper noun or adjective, 13
Punctuation, 64–65, 79–84, 121–127
  adverb clause, 131–132
  apostrophe, 106–108, 124–125
  colon, 125–127
  comma, 62, 65, 81–83
  dash, 84
  end marks, 79–80
  essential/nonessential clause, 135
  exclamation point, 74, 79
  italics (underlining), 125
  modern, 126–127
  parentheses, 84
  period, 79, 80
  question mark, 80
  quotation marks, 121–125
  semicolon, 59, 65, 83

Q

Question, 73–74
  formal terminology, 75
  formation of, 75–76
  punctuation, 80
Question mark, 80
Questions: 5 W's and an H, 85–90
Quotation marks, 121–125

R

Raise, rise, 155–156
Reading, help from grammar, 19, 83,
    85–90, 123
Reflexive pronouns, 169
Regular comparison, 175–176
Regular verb, 21–22

Relative adjective, adverb, 135–137
Relative pronoun, 133
Retained object, 104
Run-on sentence, 83, 189

S

Semicolon, 59, 65, 83
Sentence
  classified by purpose, 74–75
  command = imperative, 75
  complements, 29–32
  complex, defined, 130
  compound, defined, 59
  exclamation = exclamatory, 75
  fragment, 188–189
  main subject of, 16, 18
  main verb of, 18–19
  natural or normal order, 72, 73, 94
  question = interrogative, 75
  run-on, 83, 189
  statement = declarative, 74
  transposed order, 72, 73
Series, 60, 81
Simple sentence, 59
Sit, set, 155–156
Statement, 73
  change into question, 75–76
  formal terminology, 75
  punctuation, 79–80
State-of-being verb (*be*), 91–99
Subject (of sentence), 15–16
  agreement with verb, 170–173
  compound, 59, 171–172
  defined, 16, 18
  how to find, 16, 19
  natural or normal order, 72, 73,
      94
  pronoun, nominative case, 101
  in sentences beginning with *There*,
      94–95
  transposed order, 72, 73
  understood, 73
Subjective complement, defined, 31
Subject-verb agreement, 170–173
Subjunctive mood, 152–154

Subordinate clause
  adjective clause, 132–139
  adverb clause, 130–132
  defined, 130
  distinguished from independent
    clause, 129–130
  essential/nonessential, 135
  noun clause, 139–143
  punctuation of, 131–132
Subordinating conjunction, 130
Superlative, degree of comparison,
    175, 178–179

T

Tense, 21–27
  chart of, 22, 23
  defined, 21
  formed with *be*, 91–92
  progressive forms, 95–97
There
  compared with *their, they're*, 183
  as expletive, 94–95
Too, to, two, 183
Transitive verb
  defined, 30
  with passive voice, 98
Transposed word order, 72

U

Usage
  common problems, 25, 46, 54,
    61–62, 75–76, 102, 107–109,
    112–113, 114–115, 119, 177
  questions of usage, 163–173
  verbs causing confusion, 155–159

V

Verb(s), 17–20, 21–25, 29–31, 91–99,
    109–116, 151–162
  action, 17
  active voice, 97
  agreement with subject, 170–173
  auxiliary = helping, 24
  defined, 17, 67
  intransitive, 30, 94
  irregular, 23–24, 27, 157–158
  lie, lay, 155–156
  linking, 31, 92–94
  mood, 152–154
  normal order, 72, 73, 94
  number, 26–27
  passive voice, 97–99
  principal parts, 21–25
  progressive forms, 95–97, 109
  regular, 21–22
  rise, raise, 155–156
  sit, set, 155–156
  special problems, 155–159
  tense, 21–27
  transitive, 30
Verbals, 109–120
  dangling infinitive, 116
  dangling participle, 113
  gerund, 113–114
  infinitive, 115–119
  participle as adjective, 110
  past participle, 109
  present participle, 96, 109
  split infinitive, 160–161
Voice, active and passive, 97–99

W

Who, what, when, where, why, and
  how, 85–90
Who, whom, 76–77, 134–135
Word order, 71–77, 102, 143
  how change affects purpose, 75–77
  normal or natural, 71–72, 73
  transposed, 72
Writing well
  rules for, 189–191
  samples of, 191–193

Y

You, as understood subject, 73